CW00543135

Chanten —
the
Gnostic's Cosmos

Molana Shah Maghsoud Sadegh Angha
"Pir Oveyssi"

Translated from the original Persian by
Avideh Shashaani, Ph.D

M.T.O. SHAHMAGHSOUDI® PUBLICATIONS
Riverside, CA

M.T.O. Shahmaghsoudi® Publications

Angha, Molana Shah Maghsoud Sadegh

Chanteh — The Gnostic's Cosmos

Copyright © 1998 by Maktab Tarighat Oveyssi Shahmaghsoudi *(School of Islamic Sufism)*®. All rights reserved — copyright throughout the world. No part of this publication may be reproduced, distributed, or stored in a database or retrieval system, or transmitted in any form, whatsoever, by any means, electronic or mechanical, including photocopy, recording, without the express written consent of holder of copyright, the President of M.T.O. Shahmaghsoudi.

Library of Congress Catalog Card Number: 98-060573
ISBN: 0-910735-77-8

Printed in the U.S.A.

Published by M.T.O. Shahmaghsoudi
Printing and Publication Center
10590 Magnolia Ave., Suite G
Riverside, CA 92505   U.S.A.
e-mail: angha_rs@pacbell.net
1-800-830-0320

M.T.O. Shahmaghsoudi Headquarters
5225 Wisconsin Ave., N.W., Suite 502
Washington, D.C. 20015 U.S.A.
e-mail: mtos@cais.com
1-800-820-2180

website: http://mto.shahmaghsoudi.org

First Edition Published:
February 4th 1999

Molana Shah Maghsoud Sadegh Angha
"Pir Oveyssi"

Contents

By the same author:

The Mystery of Humanity

Ghazaliat

Manifestations of Thought

Dawn

Al-Rasa'el

Theory of Particle Structure
(the epic of life)

Al-Salat: The Reality of Prayer In Islam

Note on Gender

In translating from the Persian, the masculine gender is used in references to God and human being ("insan"). This is partly for convenience but also because the Persian language has no distinct gender denominations; thus, the Persian pronoun "ū" may mean "it", "he" as well as "she" with the proper meaning contextually determined.

Note on Transliteration

The transliteration of Arabic and Persian words follows
that of the *International Journal of Middle East Studies,*
except for the ḍād, ṭā, ṣād, and ẓāl, which are always rendered as d, t, s, and z.

The tā marbūta becomes -a except in construct where
it becomes -at.

Long vowels are indicated with a line on top.

Author's Biography

hanteh—The Gnostic's Cosmos was written in 1940 by Molana Shah Maghsoud Sadegh Angha when he was only thirty-four years old. He was the forty-first Sufi Master of Maktab Tarighat Oveyssi Shah Maghsoudi (School of Islamic Sufism) in an unbroken line of succession dating back 1400 years to the time of the Prophet Muḥammad.[1] Born in Tehran, Iran, on February 4, 1916, his heritage was physical as well as spiritual, for both his father and grandfather were themselves Sufi Masters of the order. The title "Professor" was given to Molana Shah Maghsoud Sadegh Angha by his western students to emphasize his masterful teaching of variegated topics of Sufism. Traditionally, in Persian Sufism, grand masters of Sufi orders receive honorific titles, such as *Shaykh, Pīr, Quṭb, Mawlāna, Murshid Kāmil,* or *ʿAlāmeh* (learned scholar). Among his Persian-speaking followers, his most widely used epithet is Molana al-Moazzam Hazrat (our most eminent Master).

---

1. The genealogy is included in Appendix I.

v

Professor Angha's training in the metaphysical sciences began when he was a child under his father's strict tutelage, and lasted for more than 30 years. A veritable "Renaissance" man in the breadth and depth of his interests and knowledge, he studied law, philosophy, mathematics, literature, physics and chemistry. He also studied relativity theory, astronomy (he operated his own observatory near Tehran), quantum mechanics, nuclear physics, physical chemistry and biochemistry. He was an expert in the science of alchemy and the science of letters and numbers *(jafr)*.[2]

Professor Angha revolutionized Sufism by introducing the "language" of scientific discourse in his writings, and made Sufism accessible to the scientific community. His facility in the sciences enabled him to communicate to scientists the depth and significance of the message of the Prophets. The main thrust of his teaching was directed toward providing a language and method to help people to discover their true, infinite and eternal identity. The following quote underlines this point:

> The smallest aspect of truth cannot be known through the mind and senses because the mind and the senses are in a continuous state of change in their interaction with the volatile physical environment and its relativities. Therefore, it is essential to discover and know the true place for this truth, which is the constant identity

2. Ronald Grisell, cited in the Preface of the *Hidden Angles Of Life* by Molana Shah Maghsoud Sadegh Angha. (Ponoma, CA: Multidisciplinary Publications, 1975), p.4.

and becomes associated with every being, upon his or her manifestation as a being. Since the essence of these goals is in the abstract, there must be an abstract unit at harmony with it, for its search and cognition, to make discovery possible. The reason is this: **Principles that are used in limitation are not the means for the discovery of the infinite.**[3]

Scientists such as Ronald Grisell, and Yoshimichi Maeda, who had the opportunity to meet with Professor Angha, were amazed at the breadth of his knowledge. Dr. Grisell writes in the Preface to *The Hidden Angles of Life*,

[Professor Angha] has had extensive experience in physics; particularly relativity theory, astrophysics, and nuclear physics (and operates an astronomy observatory near Teheran); in physical chemistry, biochemistry and Iranian alchemy (although the latter is not generally regarded as a science in the West) and in life sciences quite broadly. [...] In addition to science, his background contains a large portion of philosophy. Moreover, he has written several books of poetry after the grand Iranian tradition of Hafiz and Saadi. He is thus a man of many facets and a scientific "generalist" — a rare breed these centuries.[4]

As an example of his scientific acumen, one of Professor Angha's students, Sirus Aryainejad, professor of physics at Eastern Illinois University, has recently published a book entitled, *Professor Angha's Theory of Particle Structure*

3. Molana-al-Moazzam Hazrat Shah Maghsoud Sadegh Angha, *Dawn* (Lanham, MD: University Press of America, 1989), p. 29.
4. *The Hidden Angles of Life*, p. 5.

and its Applications — The Epic of Life based on the personal teachings he had received on the topic from Professor Angha.[5]

Surrounded by the spiritual tradition and heritage of Sufism and Persian westernized intellectual culture, he traveled and lectured extensively, and wrote prolifically in Farsi and Arabic. He was frequently invited as a distinguished guest scholar to speak on a various issues dealing with Sufism and Islam. Prominent scientists and scholars would visit him and have extensive discussions on matters of mutual interest. On one of his travels, he delivered a series of lectures at the Al-Azhar University in Egypt. These four treatises, *The Purification and Enlightenment of Hearts, The States of Enlightenment, Al-Salat* [Prayer], and *The Light of Salvation,* were published under the title of *Al-Rasa'el.*[6]

Knowledgeable in and appreciative of the traditional arts and crafts, he conceived the Oveyssi Sufi center in Karaj (40 kilometers northwest of Tehran) called "Sufi Abad". The center was constructed by the students of the order under the supervision of his son, Molana Hazrat Salaheddin Ali Nader Shah Angha, from 1972-78.

Sufi Abad has been closed since the Iranian Revolution. Sufi Abad is situated in spacious, green, tree-studded

5. Sadegh Angha and Sirus Aryainejad, *Professor Sadegh Angha's Theory of Particle Structure and Its Applications.* New York: Vantage Press.
6. Molana-al-Moazzam Hazrat Shah Maghsoud Sadegh-ibn-Mohammad Angha, *Al-Rasa'el.* (Lanham, MD: University Press of America), 1986.

grounds containing several large brick buildings as well as a number of smaller houses for students. The *khāniqa* is the building where Professor Angha would conduct religious services as well as seminars, meditation and chanting services. Portraits of the masters of the order, Qurʾānic calligraphy, as well as sayings from great Sufis adorn the walls. Next to the *khāniqa* is the library which houses a collection of approximately 12,000 scientific, literary, philosophical, and religious books. There is also a priceless collection of old manuscripts by Sufi Masters in Persian and Arabic. Adjacent to the library are individual chapels for prayer and meditation. Students who had achieved a certain level of spiritual progress would receive individual instruction from Professor Angha and usually spend forty days of meditation and prayer in the chapel. Close to the library is the *Kymya* (alchemy) laboratory, where the most advanced students were instructed by Professor Angha.

Also nearby is a traditional Persian bath, with marble floors and walls decorated with ceramic tiles of colorful Persian patterns and calligraphy. At the entrance is a flowing fountain surrounded by raised marble platforms used as a sitting area. Here, students who were to be initiated bathed their bodies outwardly and their souls inwardly in preparation of the initiation ceremony. At the center of the grounds is an octagonal, blue-domed museum. The architecture and interior design of the museum were developed in accordance with the science of *jafr* (science of letters and numbers) which is based on the esoteric knowledge of the Qurʾān. The shape of the dome represents Allāh as written in Arabic, and its curved sides join to form a pointed summit, representing the one point, one source, one unity. Entering the museum, sixteen large tableaus present the line of succession of the masters of the Oveyssi order, inscribed in gold on ceramic tiles. Four fine carpets, exquisite works of art, immediately attract the eye. These beautiful carpets are all hand-woven by students of the order. The painting on the ceiling is the work of the famous Iranian painter Boroujeni, depicting the stages of human existence-earthly birth, spiritual development, and divine birth. The museum houses examples of the finest arts and crafts. Found here, in addition to the fine carpets and mosaic tiles with gold, are intricate carvings, inlay work, embossment, enamel work, stained glass, carved and painted stucco, mirror mosaics, carved plaster, block printed cottons and painted textiles, miniature paintings, pottery, metal and marble engraving, and other traditional Islamic arts and crafts.

The doors of the museum open into a garden-like open patio where Professor Angha would speak individually with students. On the way out, opposite the *khāniqa*, is a small building. On the top floor is Professor Angha's meditation room and his astronomy observatory, where he would spend most of the nights observing the heavens.

During his life, Professor Angha wrote more than 150 works of poetry and prose.[7] Among them, *Manifestations of*

Thought, Ghazaliat, The Mystery of Humanity, Al-Rasa'el, The Traditional Medicine of Persia, Dawn, Al-Salat and *The Hidden Angles of Life* have been translated into English. Many of his works have also been translated in Arabic, French, German, Italian, and Spanish. From the vibrant imagery of the poems in *Ghazaliat* to the complex reasoning theory of particle structures in *The Epic of Life*, his writings reflect his depth of knowledge and his vision of life. He says in *The Epic of Life*, "I intend to open the gates of knowledge to human generations." Dr. E. Shata, Professor of Literature at the University of Cairo, writes: "During many sessions I had with Professor Angha — and each meeting was protracted hours and hours — I never felt fatigue, because his extraordinary spiritual expansion and his boundless knowledge distinguished him very clearly. He opened vast passages of various specialties like a new world to me."[8]

On September 4, 1970, Professor Angha appointed his son, Molana Salaheddin Ali Nader Shah Angha as his successor and the forty-second Master of the order. In 1978, one year before the Iranian Revolution, Professor Angha moved to San Rafael, California with his family where he continued to teach in the same tradition as in Iran. There, he passed away on November 17, 1980. He has been succeeded by his son, Molana Hazrat Salaheddin Ali Nader Shah Angha.

---

7. A listing of his major works is included in Appendix II.
8. Quoted in "Introduction," in *Dawn*, p. 5.

Chanteh's Poetic Style

Chanteh is written in the ʿ*urafā's* (gnostics') favorite classic form of *mathnawī*, which was made famous by the world-renowned Sufi, Jalāl al-Dīn Rūmī (1201-1273 CE). The *mathnawī* is generally used for long poems, sometimes consisting of thousands of lines, such as the *Mathnawī* of Rūmī. It is a verse form best suited for long, didactic, epic, romantic epic, historical, pedagogical, and related subjects. It is similar to the "doublet" used in narrative poems of the West, such as the *Canterbury Tales* and *Chanson de Geste*. It is a straight forward form, each line consisting of two hemistichs, or half-lines, rhyming together and independently of the other lines. The *mathnawī* of *Chanteh* is in the sexameter *Ramal-i Musaddā-i Maḥdhūf*, where each hemistich is three feet in length: $^{\circ}$Ä$\cup$— |Ä$\cup$—|–$\cup$–$^{\circ}$. In the last line — here the third — two short syllables may take the place of a long one, thus, $^{3}\cup\cup$–^{3}, or ^{3}Ä^{3} are accepted only as the "final" feet of hemistichs. The meter is *maḥdhūf*, i.e., "cut", or, "truncated" because the last foot is shorter in length by one syllable. Each *mathnawī* is only internally rhymed, without any limitations on the number of lines the poet may wish to compose. For example, Rūmī's *Mathnawī*, is ca. 65,000 lines; Firdawsī's *mathnawī*, the *Shāhnāma*, ca. 70,000 lines; Nizāmī's *mathnawīs* in his Quintet, e.g. *Layli and Majnun, Farhad and Shirin*, etc. are ca. 5,000 lines long. Sanāʿī's five *mathnawīs* — the first and the model for ʿ*irfān* poetry-are more than 7,000 lines each.

Chanteh departs from the classical *mathnawīs* by adding a half-line after every proper *mathnawīs* line. However, each of the 1,206 of these half-lines are also in the Classical meter *Ramal-i Musaddā-i Maḥdhūf*. The third half-line of every main numbered line includes a semantic level of signification not immediately obvious. Many of these are explanations of the line above them; others, at their ordinary level of signification are seemingly "out of place" — perceived as adding almost nothing to the intended and conveyed "meaning" of the line. But, almost as Japanese Haiku poetry, as well as the poetry of other cultures, they are not mere additions of a half-line poem for no reason. They are meant to intimate in the reader a reality that does not fit "words" and "phrases". They are meant for study, contemplation and reflection. They must be internalized, together with *Chanteh* as a whole. Some are truly enigmatic, and the English translation has made every attempt to preserve this quality.

Chanteh and Its Significance

Written in verse, *Chanteh — The Gnostic's Cosmos* is a masterful synthesis of metaphysics and physics. In *Chanteh*, the author aims at harmonizing science and the principles of the science of *ʿirfān*. It shows *ʿirfān* as a scientific endeavor and as a method of attaining certitude in knowledge. The author writes in his introduction that he intends to clarify the misunderstanding that exists between physics and metaphysics, and "[...] explain the reality of nature in its true and unlimited scope."

Chanteh uses the language of Persian poetic discourse to present the holistic and intuitive cognizance of reality which includes physics and metaphysical principles. The language of poetic discourse is usually not the best language to present scientific problems such as: Ordinal & Cardinal One, Typology of One, Concept of Numeric "Order", Potential Infinite and the Impossibility of the Actual Infinite, Invalidity of Infinite Regression, etc. However, the author's success in combining his knowledge of mathematics with poetry is partly due to his use of the thousand year old meta-language of poetry and prose, along with his in-depth knowledge of philosophy and sciences.

Chanteh is a probing discourse on complex issues which may collectively be named "religious philosophy", or "mystical philosophy". It is a theoretical work that assumes a high level of knowledge on the part of the reader concerning the philosophical-mystical foundations of Sufism as it has developed in Iran and has been presented in Persian both in poetry and prose. *Chanteh* is a work which engages the reader to think along. It is not a literary poem as such. The form of the work — the *mathnawī* — is the same as Rūmī's best-known work in English, the *Mathnawī*.

However, Rūmī's more theoretical works have not been translated into English (e.g. the probing odes of the *Divān-e Kabīr* or the prose work *Fīhi mā Fīhi*). Rūmī is primarily a mystical poet whose *Mathnawī* is a populist didactic work that cannot be characterized as a work on the philosophical foundations of mysticism. Although *Chanteh* is didactic on one level, the author is mainly concerned with problems pertaining to the foundations of knowledge. His aim is to demonstrate the harmony of the epistemological foundations of mysticism and the science of metaphysics. *Chanteh* is not a populist work as the author is probing mainly philosophical issues of the epistemology of scientific and mystical knowledge.

If one compares *Chanteh* with literature in the non-Persian tradition, one realizes that, in terms of topics covered and methodology employed, *Chanteh's* principle is most similar to the Aristotelian method, while its overall findings concerning the foundations of knowledge are close to Platonism. Specifically, *Chanteh* combines the methodology of Aristotle's *Posterior Analytics* and his theories of intellectual knowledge as presented in *Metaphysics XII* and *De Anima III*, with Plato's ideas on "Intellectual Knowledge" (7th letter) and "Innate Knowledge," which is to be "remembered" or "recovered" within the soul. Here, Platonic theories of self and immortality (*Crito* and *Phaedo*) may be compared to Professor Angha's views. Certainly the philosophical level of *Chanteh* is more along the lines of Islamic peripatecism and Platonicized

Illuminationist Philosophy than with the populist styles of Rūmī's *Mathnawī*. The Persian tradition of mystical philosophy stands on its own. Its roots are manyfold: Islamic Peripatetic philosophy, Illuminationist philosophy, as well as the long tradition of mystical theories on the soul and knowledge, on being and knowing, which may be seen as mystical refinements of strict philosophical approaches to the analysis of problems pertaining to the foundations of epistemology and psychology. *Chanteh* is Persian poetry, but its meta-language of discourse is similar to the mytho-poetic language of the Platonic Dialogues, and its theoretical approach is more similar to Aristotle than to less theory-oriented mystical works. It is not a populist religious, nor popular mystical work. It can be characterized as "philosophy of mysticism".

To understand *Chanteh* one must understand Sufism. *Chanteh* employs a specific discourse which itself must be seen through the history of the development of theoretical Sufism, or what is best described as Persian Speculative Gnosis.

The epistemological theory upon which *Chanteh* rests is known as "Knowledge by Presence". This is a type of intuitive holistic knowledge of principles which may be observed and re-observed, and thus re-formulated at any time by using meta-language. *Chanteh* is a prime example of this theory incorporated within a complete work in some 400 lines of poetry. But the author at every step relies on his topic's intuitive linkage with holistic reality. One has to know Sufism to explain: 1- praxis, which includes *zuhd, warāʾ, ṭalab, hayra,* all the way to *fanāʾ;* and 2- theory, which is philosophy and has two components, Aristotelian of the Islamic Peripatetics (al-Farabī and Avicenna) and Illuminationist (Suhrawardī and especially the *Ḥikmat-i Mutaʾallihi* of Sabziwārī). Together, they form a special metaphysics which is more Platonic in principle, and places a primary emphasis on intuitive philosophy over and beyond discursive philosophy. Thus, the author is able to explain mystical phenomena such as inner experience, true dreams, and visions.

The term *chanteh* is a Persian term with at least two levels of signification. In ordinary language it signifies a "pouch", or "one's possessions". In the language of Gnostic discourse, the term has at least two different meanings: It refers either to a person's spiritual discoveries obtained through praxis, or to the sum total of a mystic's visionary knowledge as well as the discursive knowledge he/she has gained through study. In this context, the term chanteh signifies the quintessence of what the author has to offer in regard to both visionary and discursive knowledge of Reality. We may here call it a symbol and, as with all symbols, the term *chanteh* is not given to translation into another language, except at an ordinary level of signification. In sum, the term chanteh expresses the author's own experience, plus his attempt to communicate it through the medium of poetry.

Professor Angha's *Chanteh* is not merely a formal, proper, acceptable Persian *mathnawī*. It is much more. The formal aspect is but a thin outer layer-perhaps even a disguise-of a veritable, deep, thought provoking and "original" manifold "Gnostic's Cosmos".

The text itself is quite distinctly written in the best 13th century tradition of Persian mysticism. Subsequent to the introduction of Plato's mytho-poetic style of his *Dialogues*, as well as intellectual *Peripateticism*, two textual traditions followed: Aḥmad Ghazzālī's *Sawāniḥ* which continues through ʿAyn al-Qudhāt al-Hamadānī, Rūzbihān Baqlī Shīrāzī, et. al., and Sanāʿī's intellectual *Gnosticism* composed entirely in the *mathnawī* form. This latter branch continues with ʿAṭṭār, reaches its apogee with Rūmī and continues with such mystics as Shabistārī (author of *Gulshān-i Raz*), Shāh Niʿmattullah Wālī, and many other notable Gnostics who wrote works on the same set of timeless questions about being, becoming, and passing, until the present.

Chanteh, in its form of *mathnawī*, as well as from the standpoint of intellectual aims and somewhat didactic nature, falls within the second category. Most of the authors of this category are not primarily concerned with poetic form and style. They are not poets *per se*, such as Rudakī, Saʿdī, and Bahar. Rūmī, for example, even ridicules the poets that are so preoccupied with form that they become oblivious to the meaning conveyed by their compositions.

Like his predecessors, the author of *Chanteh* employs the poetic medium as a tool. For him poetry is the *telos* of thinking and the best suited medium to communicate visionary experiential knowledge. He even attempts to convey the indescribable side of it — that which is apprehended through variegated channels, such as dreams, visions and inspirations, yet not readily given to description, nor ever easily communicated as-it-is to someone else. This is the quintessential message of Persian poetic wisdom. The phrase, *yudraku wa lā yūsaf* (it is apprehended but not describable) alludes to this issue. And *Chanteh* is all about a monumental effort to describe, and not to deny, communication of the subjective experience of holistic Reality — to make every earnest effort to convey the supreme ecstasy of the experience of knowledge to others.

Avideh Shashaani, Ph.D.
February 4, 1998

Author's Introduction

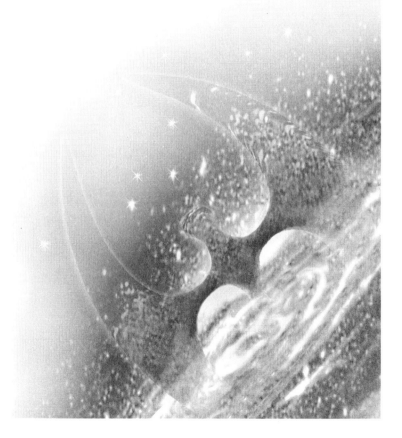

This Chanteh, this overflowing treasure-house,

Contains the key to divine treasure

'Tis the grace of Ghotbeddin Mohammad,

'Tis his knowledge of limitless Truth,
thus inspired.

Hova Allah-o'l-ʿAli[1]

(HE, GOD the Exalted)

Introduction

*I*nfinite nature is the harmonious manifestation of self-reality; or, the Principle of Being. Principles of knowledge are more fundamental, necessary and timeless, than knowledge gained solely based on experimental discoveries of different eras. This is because during each period, knowledge of nature depends upon methods available to humans. Thus scientific laws and principles are not true forever. Those laws which are more lasting are derived from rules which are closest to, as derived from principles innate[2] in being.[3]

1. This Arabic phrase appears in numerous different contexts in Islam, such as at the end of the "call to prayer" (*Adhān*), in the *rakʿas* of the daily prayer (optional), at the commencement of rituals as well as at their terminus, as the opening line of books, and in numerous other contexts. The phrase is one of the most common formulaic exaltations of God.
2. "Innate": equivalent of the Arabic *fitra*, is a *Qurʾānic* term, and appears in various derivatives of the triliteral verb *f-t-r*; also as *fitra* — the verbal noun of the basic verb (*Sūrat al-Anʿām*: VI, *āya*, 79 — with the basic meaning "God Created"), in some 15 *āyas*, mostly with meanings signifying variations on acts of creation and the ensuing effects. In one *āya* (*Sūrat al-Rūm*: XXX, *āya*, 30) in

5

If self-constituted knowledge may seem astonishing and awesome, to an individual, a society, and to the earth's inhabitants, it is yet of little significance when compared to the knowledge of infinite nature.[4]

The prominent scientists of the world have, according to their understanding, recognized the true greatness of nature, and have acknowledged their own insignificance relative to great sages, who search with an aspirant spirit and an investigative mind in order to discover the secrets of nature. To their sensitive minds, even the smallest manifestations are significant. They believe that whatever has "appearance"[5] has "meaning," and each manifestation is a

construct with "humans", *fitrat al-nās*, the meaning of "innate disposition" is both clear and unique: "what God gave to a human when He created him/her." However, the term *fitra* and together with *seresht* — its Persian equivalent — occupy a special place in Iranian intellectual history: in *fiqh*, *tafsīr*, *kalām*, *usūl*, *falsafa*, and *tasawwuf*. It signifies that the whole cosmos has, within its essence, an innate disposition to know.

3. The problem stated is one of the most significant and lasting problems of the philosophy of science. From the pre-Socratic times, to Plato and Aristotle, to early Medieval peripatetics, such as Alfarabi, Avicenna, and Averroës, to the later Latin philosophers — the quintessence of which is to be found in St. Thomas Aquinas' (1224/5-1274), *Summa Theologicæ*, ed. Thomas Gilby (London, 1963-75), 60 vols.

4. Self-constituted knowledge if/when experienced by the human may, (if and only if the individual has gained the necessary learning to recognize the experience) change that individual's self, the objects sought, and the perception of reality, and will be shocked by the enormity of God-human "relation." Sufism teaches to recognize and apprehend the meta-language of Persian *ʿirfān-i nazarī* — together with its multiple levels of semantic signification.

5. "Appearance" is the "*Evidenz*" (see fn. 76) of a thing-in-itself, which, barring any obstacle may be seen in outer reality by a sound eye and immediately recognized for what it is. The terms *ibsār* and *dīdan* apply, but anything outside the visible range may also be "seen". Here the term *Mushāhada* applies. Thus a unified theory of "Seeing and Vision" which gains valid results (the thing seen as is) in the entire range of continuum reality.

form of reality. Perhaps, it is this very thought that has limited the followers of the school of Idealism to take steps beyond the limited. Yet, unfounded deviations are not sufficient to completely obstruct the Truth.

To suppose that the discovery of endless scientific laws is dependent on the passage of time, or for an appropriate time in the future, is a naïve and unacceptable view before foresighted minds. It is more valid to say that the reality of existence in presenting itself in its unbounded [continuous] natural forms has informed us of the closest means of perception. It is, however, this closeness which has given rise to misconceptions; but those who are able to comprehend realities with facility are those whose senses are more receptive in accepting the innate harmony with the multitude of evident [thus "seeable"] manifestations.

If we study the biographies of scientists, we will discern that they are cognizant of and value the truth above all. They are, in effect, the true observers of the realm of being. With simple observations of nature, scientists have been able to make discoveries; it is the smallest and the most simple manifestations of nature which comprise the subject of their reflection and thus the basis of their findings.

For example, Newton (1642-1727), the renowned English scientist, discovered the law of gravitation by first observing a falling apple. Galileo, in observing a moving church lantern, discovered the formula for the pendulum; thereafter he continued to discover other laws governing natural phenomena. Hence, it can readily be accepted that scientists, whose sensitive systems have not been subjected to baseless illusions, are in effect concerned only with the validity and truth of being.

It is surprising to note how some philosophers have stopped at the mere observance of nature and have digressed from pursuing correct knowledge of the truth of being [by accepting imposed limits of archaic methodologies]. Although nature itself is the most evident expression of reality, yet some [natural] philosophers have been satisfied only with appearances and with manifestations [in outer reality]; and furthermore have considered the limited effects [they see] to be reality itself.

It is my intention in this treatise to lift the imaginary boundary created by a minor misconception relating physics and metaphysics; and I further aim to explain the reality of nature in its true and unlimited scope.[6] In this brief introduction, I have not considered it necessary to write my own biography, for I am certain that true scholars will perceive and distinguish my identity through the sensitive aspects of my thoughts represented in my writings. For, it is said, "Man is hidden behind his thoughts." Those scientific

6. The author here aims to clarify two things: 1- A most common misconception even among learned scholars, who confuse ʿilm-i kullī with some kind of "universal knowledge". 2- Principles of physics are not to be sought in and through material physics, but from the "physics" of things non-corporeal which, however, "move", are "coordinated", are "shaped", etc. and exist in the whole continuum reality — entities which may act as "cause", be an "effect", etc.

truths which are carefully discerned will be invaluable for the seekers of truth.

The significant source which has acquainted and guided me to this method of thinking has been the training of my wise and learned father, whose true self is one of the great mysteries. His vigilant wisdom, as infinite rays of light, continuously guide and enfold me. My joy and contentment may be considered a subtle and sincere token of my gratitude. It is his unconditional and endless generosity that has allowed me to proceed with my duties thus to reap the harvest from his inspiring spirit as much as possible.

Although receptive souls during the course of time should have the capability of receiving truth, being trained by a learned teacher does not necessarily require a long time nor depend on lengthy discourses. Rather, the brief yet penetrating words of the wise teacher have been the ever-illuminating beacons along long and dark paths. Such words uttered are unto listeners as doors, which if opened, will allow initiated individuals to witness immense gardens in realms spiritual and allow them to behold its nourishing fruits.

I must say that each of my teacher's instructions bestowed on me during a lifetime of sincere devotion and constant companionship, have controlled my senses and have enhanced my innate "hearing"[7] ability. And, whenever by necessity those melodies are repeated, each one reveals a new mystery to me. How abundant and precious are true and everlasting blessings-the eternal protector of grateful souls.

Brighter than the moon is my star
The sun is but mere dust at the door of my existence
I am pure spirit and time's Jesus
Pay heed, Father's grace is upon me.

---

7. "Innate hearing", just as "innate seeing", etc. are all instruments that lead to knowledge not limited by any and all types of bodily, sentimental, ethical, societal, custom, etc. Cf. Plato's concept of "recalling", or "remembering."

Poetic Introduction

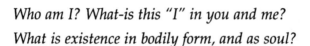

Who am I? What-is this "I" in you and me?
What is existence in bodily form, and as soul?

What-is "I", never repeated?
What is the pith of my life?

Is our life limited to corporeal body?
Or, will I exist after death?

Is it I or He, my essence?
Or, is our essence limited to the body?

To discover creation's temporal flux
Will equivocal arguments satisfy the mind?

Is knowledge what is reaped by the senses?
Obtained by man purely through
*   sense-perception and by analogy?*

Or, does man possess an essence eternal?
For which existence-evident itself is proof?

Is reality only perceived and thus caused?
Is man merely corporeal, soul-less body?

Can forms perceived come to be independent
of prior thought?
Or, is the order apparent when manifest
knowledge is seen?

Are the manifest flux signs of some prior Essence.
Or, is there nothing but matter and substance?

Is Being a continuum, or is it discrete?
What determines dimensions of the whole-reality?

Can Absolute Essence be perceived
*   by sense perception?*
Or, is cosmic order devoid of design and order?

What negligent reason perceives chaos?
Why tension, dichotomy, and tumult;
*   if Existence is one?*

By God's will, 'Tis words of truth
Gushing forth from the core upon this writ.

Though the learned of yesteryears oft have said,
Many a jewel have they shaped out of truth,
*   sifted and strung to merge as one.*

But small as an ant am I, my offering apt in size,
And an ant's bequest must fit the nest.

Yet my Guide is the Cosmic City of Knowledge,
From where guides Jesus glorious,
  with sanctified Breath.

Through Muḥammad Revelation was brought to us,
  and hear it indeed we did.
A confidant are you? I didn't utter a secret point.
  Be silent![8]

By virtue of Solomon's radiating Knowledge I, too,
  have become solid,
As a mountain. Alas! Though he whisked me away
  as a strand of straw.

---

8. "Silent", *khamūsh*, is one of Rūmī's poetic names (*takhallus*). The author makes an obvious reverent gesture to Sufism's undisputed Master of Masters, and *axio mundi* of the age.

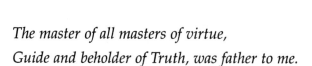

The master of all masters of virtue,
Guide and beholder of Truth, was father to me.

He is the Gate of Knowledge,[9] and God's epiphany,
Leader and guide unto lovers of God.

In Sufism's ocean, he is cognition's whale,
And the principal perceived attribute
       of God's Essence.[10]

He is the Treasure-House of grace and generosity,
In truth, his hand is an instrument of the
       Hand of God.

9. Reference is made to a widely known and commonly repeated *Hadīth* (oral tradition of the Prophet Muḥammad), "I am the City of Knowledge, and ʿAlī is its Gate."

10. The jurists equate attributes with the Qurʾānic "99 Names" of God, and assert that the theological question has a principle validity based on the authority of Revealed Law. Thus, and according to this specific juridical and theological view, Allah is a unity indicated by the sum of His Attributes which then indicate the Essence.

He is knowledge and perception's fathom-less ocean,
Uttering secrets, absolved of the limitations of
sounds and words.

His proclamations — heart's revelation —
does intoxicate,
Thus puts Avicenna to shame for the inadequacies
of his book, The Directives.[11]

Witness the pure Essence of God, is he,
Lover of God, the path and guide, is he.

Secrets of inner meanings, did he divulge to us,
Many such wisdom's pearls did he pierce.

---

11. Reference is made to Avicenna's gnostic, ʿirfān-ī, philosophical work, *al-Ishārāt wa al-Tanbīhāt* (*The Directives and Remarks*). "Ishārāt" stands for "allusion" — signs and symbols of Gnostic truths, and "*Tanbīhāt*" signifies "admonitions," to those seekers of Truth.

From what my Master did bestow,
My soul fell upon the Treasure-House of knowledge.

It is not I, who speaks, it is he from the midst,
In truth, 'tis he the kernel, and I the shell.

His love has made me radiate,
And now my body has found undying soul.

You, the Guide! Love of souls truthful,
We are mere dust at the threshold of the Abode.

From you, my soul has guidance sought,
What I write is all your eloquent words.

'Tis from you we seek; return O Master!
'Tis your aid, in spirit's realm, that divulges the way.

Poetic Interlude

Molana Mir Ghotbeddin
Mohammad Angha

"Pir Oveyssi"

He, the Exalted Lord God

Guidance Real
By the emanations of
The Great Pir and Teacher Hazrat Mir
Ghotbeddin Mohammad Angha,
"Pir Oveyssi"

O you, who have not reached out for
  the Beloved's hand,
And turned away from His command!

O you, not entrusted with the secrets of love
And thus deprived of love's divine mounts!

O you, not sought support from intellect's[12] mite,
And cast stones upon its balance right!

O you, cloaked in saintly garb,
Take on a patched robe fashioned of fish's scales,

You have looked into every grotto and ditch,
Unaware yet of mysteries that in you reside.

---

12. The "intellect" (*'aql*) functions to construct holistic systems through which valid truths are obtained. While some purely noetic rational truths may be named "wisdom," the Sufis usually do not equate the intellectual epistemic mode — also named the "rational" — alone with wisdom. "Wisdom" comes about in its highest form as the result of harmonized discursive and intuitive knowledge.

You've spent your precious life collecting words,
But hidden to you remain their meanings signified.

False beads in hand, clients your "consorts"
            in attendance
And counsel, yet, you bestow; on jewels,
            the best gem, and all.

One such foolish customer is your own heart's want,
Who surely thus inflates the value of your beads,
            pretentious and false.

Grandly you boast, as if you are Junayd's[13] Master,
Your grand wish is naught but deceit.

---

13. Junayd of Baghdad (died early 8th century C.E.), is a famous Sufi of the formative period of *Basra-Kufah* Sufism, which stressed the practice of piety (*zuhd*), abstinence (*wara'*), prayer and vigil. Hallā's famous statement, "I am the Truth" (*ana al-Haqq*) was considered blasphemous, and he was executed.

Pleased you are by the lowly throw at you in jest,
How will you be cleansed of this filth and bigotry?

Clear is not your blood, nor spite-free your flesh,
Your lofty efforts are mere worldly games.

Your value is not other than "I" and "us",
How can "I" and "us" flesh and bone signify?

The body's virtue is but to consume and use,
And feed upon earth's cycled waste.

Death is the body's concluding end,
The warmth of the action: "buy and sell",
        coldness will put to end.

Eternal existence is not bound by the body,
'Tis not bodily so to seek a corporeal shell.

'Tis immaterial body, pure and shadow-less,
Which becomes the epiphany of the essence sublime.

Existence's design is His affair,
The universe moves along His compass' trace.

As the compass began to make its turn,
The circle was made to move around its own center.

As long as words tell of absolute Existence,
No mention shall be made of "us", "I" or "you".

When the veil is dropped from our existence,
Our self-worship will be revealed.

When the soul to the body estranged becomes,
Entrusted with secrets of the Hidden Realm,
        you will be.

When body's veil be lifted from the soul,
Your being shall become annihilated in time.

'Twas illusion — your image — formed of you,
Since "appearance" is not your real being.

'Tis Essence, the light of the heaven and earth,
Each particle's propagating radiance,
> *a symbol of manifest light.*

Till your heart is not to the source connected,
Divine light will not shine upon it to illuminate.

Times cognizant you are that God is your life's source,
Yet severed is your heart from His light.

O you riddled with doubts! Your heart is dark
So 'tis distanced from the source of Light.

Whether your candle be dim, bright or ablaze,
Since there's no connection to the source,
   measure naught its radiance.

Creation is an opaque veil, blinding our vision
   of luminosity in all,
Remove the obstacle and "see" the source:
   God the One Eternal Absolute Light.

If man mirror of His countenance should be,
Glory of His Light will shine from his inner
   to the outer.

If the heart be connected to the soul of souls,
Light will flow from it and becomes one with soul.

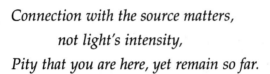

Connection with the source matters,
  not light's intensity,
Pity that you are here, yet remain so far.

When light descends from limitless,
  unqualified space,[14]
It shall rest in the forever unfolding possibility —
  the world.

The heart which is polished and absorbs light,
Illuminated will it be from the Light Divine.

The one who sold "heart" to light's colorful illusions,
Is leagues away from the Light Sublime.

---

14. The term used here is *lā makān*, which lit. means "non-space", or, space-in the Euclidean sense-negates the limits imposed by classical concepts of *peros* and *apeiros*, so axioms of one man's geometry, etc. are lifted. Thus, there is not just one-and-only-one space in our whole continuum reality. Understanding reality of such a "wonderland" space, where "laws" and our common sense do not hold, is an important "key" to unravel one of Sufism's principles of Epistemology.

If the heart's surface is not cleansed nor clear,
How can it manifest light, or be the place
for light to reach?

Reason is lame on this path,
Yet, it invites all to challenge its might.

Man relies on short-sighted reason,
Thinking it will take him beyond noetic land.

Anything wherein colors play, Light it is surely not,
Light is but the intensity of passionate attraction.

Love is illumined only from the Light of God,
Thus to be paired with Truth, and one with God.

If the heart's eye and ear should open,
Then privy it will become to this secret's treasury.

How will this eye and ear be opened unto you?
Thus to become elevated without guidance
of the Pīr?[15]

Best to bow in submission at the Pīr's door,
Best his companionship beyond any a teaching.

Many subtle truths I've said, yet no one heard,
The gnat did not become Angha's[16] *confidant.*

Close my lips, and say: "enough!"
Woe! Is there anyone here
who may fly with **Angha**?

15. *Pīr* — in Persian, the traditional title of the head of a Sufi order (*tarīqa*) endowed with the highest authority for the teaching and transmission of Gnostic insight.
16. Reference is made to the author's name and his lineage. In the Persian mythos, and in many types of literary works in New Persian, Angha is the mythical bird whose abode is the Empyrean of Almighty God, and may interfere in human life to preserve the Good.

Behold! How Father enlightened me,
In his School of Love, he made a Pīr of me.

I was water, he thrust fire unto my soul,
I was of earth, He cast me upon the wind.

Chanteh —
the
Gnostic's Cosmos

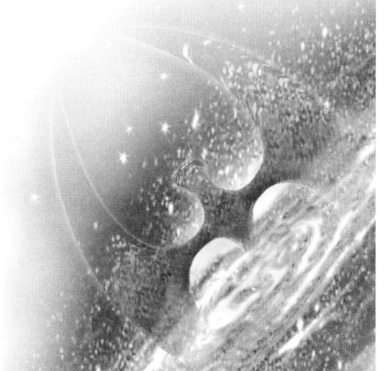

He, the Exalted Lord God

Infinite praise worthy is of God alone

Whose absolute, unrestricted

quiddity, reason[17] unaided

will never find

For He is beyond measure

17. *'Aql*, reason, *nous* in Greek, the highest rational human faculty whose truths obtained by syllogistic reasoning and demonstration, are not just valid, they are known with certitude. They are unique, since they may be objectified as valid propositions, thus communicated through "language".

Absolute in essence, beyond any analogy
Not in need of prayer, thanks, and praises
      offered unto Him
Know God the Exalted!

He who commanded "Be!"[18] *and created the worlds*
He initiated becoming, but not as ancillary to being
In such manner, He created the existents

His Throne made in the innermost sanctum
His own abode in Existence's Throne
He as soul, existence as dust

His Face He showed in the six-sided mirror
Rather, He is both the face and *mirror*
Existence and manifestation

---

18. Qurʾānic edict "Be! And thus there came to be, and the process of becoming commenced" (Qurʾān: VI: 73). In mystical philosophy, "special" humans may reach the "rank of Be!" (named, *maqām kun*).

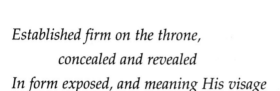

Established firm on the throne,
   concealed and revealed
In form exposed, and meaning His visage
Guard the secrets

Being is the Essence of God, without doubt
What is existence? The magnificent signs of God
Being is the essence of God

Non-existence is but the reflection of Existence
For ᶜirfān proclaims naught of Non-Being
What is non-existence in different realms?

Non-existence without doubt is not absolute
Know negating the negation, to be affirmation[19]
Name negation "confirmation"

19. One of the five primary principles of standard logic, is Aristotle's two-way logic organized in the nine-book *Organon*. But throughout history thinkers have questioned the very notion "self-evident." In post-Avicennan Illuminationist philosophy in Iran, nothing is self-evident prior to "proof." The reconstructed system, posits that the only self-evident truth is "the 'I' recognizing its self-consciousness to be valid" as the most prior cosmic "primary principle".

The secret of negation is unknown to you
'Tis positive absolute, and cannot be judged by you
Non-existence is not known to you

In nature, whatsoever you see of increase or decline
Was non-existent, and came to be out of non-being
This is the secret of pre-existence

If you find the secrets of non-existence
You will learn that the secret of existence is pure
Since you've found the King of the path

Thus, non-existence is the ocean of God's generosity
It is not non-existence, 'tis rather absolute existence
The origin of everything is God

19. One of the five primary principles of standard logic, is Aristotle's
two-way logic organized in the nine-book *Organon*. But throughout
history thinkers have questioned the very notion "self-evident." In
post-Avicennan Illuminationist philosophy in Iran, nothing is self-evident prior to "proof." The reconstructed system, posits that the only
self-evident truth is "the 'I' recognizing its self-consciousness to be
valid" as the most prior cosmic "primary principle".

He made apparent the Sufi's figure
Thus to see His own beauty in him
Don't underestimate this greatness

The image of His essence fell into non-existence
Therein, thus His essence became seeker of mirrors
Or, non-existence sought the essence

As His essence was one and unique
He fashioned His own essence unto non-existence
Remedy turned to pain within the soul

As His visage glowed in non-existence's realm
Non-existence transformed into reflector of existence
The secret of pre-existence was thus revealed

Since non-existence describes Essence's attributes
Non-existence perfect mirror unto
> *Essence thus became*
Negations all became confirmations

His single glance non-being to being turned
And man by the breath of grace thus
> *became intoxicated*
Non-being turned into existence

Thus for sure, Adam[20] pure at first was he
And, attributes of God hidden through him
The tablet of his soul is pure

---

20. Biblical name of the first human created by God. Ādam in Arabic and Persian is the name which appears in the Qurʾān in twenty five āyas (Qurʾānic verses). He is God's "Chosen One" (*al-muṣṭafā*) before whom all angels prostrate themselves by the Command of God (*amr Allāh*) save Iblīs, that is Satan.

Who is Adam? Manifestations of God's Essence
Inconceivable, incomparable, and unique
Seek unity in multiplicity

Omniscient Adam, though,
*   didn't stand for His Essence*
And, yet the best mirror reflecting God's
*   Essence, was he*
In him the Essence is present, [without sameness]

Heart is God's pure mirror
The enlightened one knows the King of the Path
For he is close to God

"Lā ilāha"[21] is the heart's pure mirror
This statement is worthy only of the perfect Pīr
To fathom every level signified is not a simple task

---

21. Reference is made to the *shahāda* (testament of faith) in Islam *"lā ilāha illā Allāh"* (there is no deity but Allah).

His inner being is absolved of the dyad "we" and "I"
Truly he is holder of the mirror reflecting God
He is free of body and soul

Should soul's mirror be cleansed of
      impurity and tarnish
Then, whatever is seen therein is the Face of God
Existence is the mirror of "lā"[22]

Know the attribute of the
      Essence as the "face in the mirror"
Know that Essence and Attribute are one,
      reflected in the mirror[23]
Cleanse the tablet of the soul

---

22. "*lā*" is part of the *shahāda* denoting negation — "not." In the context of Sufism, it means that when one negates the "self", then the "All" is the only ever-present Being.
23. The "sameness," or "unity," of God's Essence and Attributes — i.e., that He is and what He is are not differentiated — is a major theological doctrine first formulated by the "rationalist" *Muᶜtazila* dialectical theologians, whose speculative principles made a major impact on the development of *Shīᶜism* and Sufism in Iran.

So the Face of God and God are one
How can attribute be separated from Essence?
As the reverberating resonance of sound

"I was a hidden treasure"[24], His Light luminous
    on Covenant's day[25]
Is the manifestation of God's Essence real?
The enlightened are aware of this

To perceive this light manifest
Cleanse the mirror of your heart
See ʿAlī[26] in this manifestation

---

24. Reference is made to *Hadīth Qudsī* where God says, "I was a hidden treasure. I wanted to be known, therefore, I created." There have been many Sufi interpretations of this Tradition, commonly accepted to be valid throughout Islamic lands.
25. The day of covenant in Islam, *rūz-i alast* in Persian, is a reference to the Qurʾān: VIII, 172, when man accepts God's Lordship over him, and thus the covenant between God and man. Man shall obey His Commands, and God shall uphold His promises.
26. Reference is made to the fourth of the righteous Caliphs, who was the Prophet Muḥammad's cousin and son-in-law. He is the first Imam of the *Shīʿa*, and revered by most Sufis as the quintessence of mystical knowledge.

To praise God is to submit to Him
No creature exists submitted not to serving God
What can exist then, apart from God?

Questioning the Ineffable One is wrong
Describing God in fact is limiting Him
> *by our expressions*
There are no limits upon the "description" of God
> *[our language is but one limit]*

God's Essence cannot be perceived nor described
He is the Ocean of Existence, and this World
> *just the surface foaming brine*
He is beyond all such words and all statements

No one has uncovered God as God is
Even though he may have learned Socrates' wisdom
Or endeavored with scientific scrutiny

Since you are one unit, don't speak of the unlimited
Don't mislead people by resounding ignorance
Don't stir up turmoil in the world

The "one" as unit, and the principle unity
　　　of One are distinguished
The one as unit, is limited
Multiplicity is its proof

One cannot be the measure for the unlimited,
　　　nor for unity
Limitation is the boundary between one and unity
There is no limit for infinite numbers

The philosopher, too, has a path in this abode
But his is fraught with rocks and crevasses
When will you become aware of this?

The intellect employs the laws of reasoning
       to explain the now
But, we know that reason alone is a
       restraining noose
Uttered words aplenty, are this era's plague

What use describing "syrup" you have not tasted?
How can abstract reasoning allow you to
       "taste" the real?
The particular, the universal —
       they are nothing but abstract terms

Meaning can never be allocated
       by words and terms alone
Deep sea cannot fit "container" — merely a term
Do not, thus waste your time [with talk]

Since meanings are not conveyed by words
How can you "see" God by merely repeating "god"?
Even with strong proofs

Everything from "form", "body", and
       "prime matter" are but uttered words
His Essence though, free of such illusions, is real
The inner core never resembles the outer skin

Go recite! "Whoso desireth to meet God."[27]
Acquaint more your heart awakened
And, seek the path from within

Seek help in patience and prayer,
Go! Separate yourself from foolish tales
Seek stability on the path to God

27. Qurʾān: XXIX, 5.

The moment you are endowed
      with all the attributes of God
Your religion's day shall come, and all things from
      all directions will be revealed to you
You will become related, as attribute to Essence

Behold this, "To You alone we pray and from You
alone we ask for help"[28]
See the relationship between the attribute
      and the source
Go seek the perfection of religion

Constant utterance, "Guide us,"[29]
      will enlighten your heart
So, kindle the desire in your heart's eye to seek to see
Empty your heart of the estranged in this abode

28. Qurʾān: I, 4.
29. Qurʾān: I, 5.

At the moment your heart
        is illuminated by God's light
It will experience magnificent awe[30] *of "us" and "I"*
It shall become a mirror to see His Grace

Then, you shall need no other but God
You shall renounce Satan,[31]
        and embark upon the path to God
In poverty, a king you'll be

---

30. "Awe" is one of the three main senses of the experience of the numinous.
31. In Sufism, "Satan" is usually a metaphor for the carnal self. As such it is demonizing — and "dualistic", for unity and resolution is obtained only after it is done away with. Through "killing" and through "annihilation" of the carnal self rideden with satanic tension and given to demonizing control, the self may achieve "freedom", similar to the Sanskrit *moksha* and the Buddhist notion of nirvana. However, "Satan" in the Sufi tradition, beyond the metaphor, that is, at its highest level of semantic signification is not objectified, nor ever given an embodiment as in fundamentalist religion, nor even as in popular theology nor religion taken as a whole.

When heart's mirror is cleared of all obscuring dust
Then, upon it only the Beloved's reflection shall befall
So keep clear your heart's mirror

He, the Exalted Lord God

Be aware of every turn of the carnal soul
And, like the spirit,
of another realm be aware
Lest the intellect beckoned, should be
The self unto oblivion cast away,
must be.

A secret I will reveal openly to you
Pay heed as you comprehend it
Then, your heart will find peace

In the state of awe, attributes and Essence
        are one and the same
Go seek this state of awe,
            for 'tis awe that seeks the Essence
Though your awe is in you alone

Should God's self-emanating Essence engulf you
Then your awe will intensify the heart's luminosity
Tremendous perfection is the light of soul

For this reason the Master Gnostic, Rūmī
In his magnificent book, the Mathnawī, *thus stated*
In simple words

"Sell cleverness and buy awe
Cleverness is doubt and awe insight"[32]
Tear the veils [that cover the Truth]

Disputes and inquiries of the limited senses
Hinder your steps toward your goal
Your desires are mere illusions before you

On the path to God,
*   awe does relinquish all appearances*
It thus negates this world's "reality"
'Tis obliteration of all fantasies and of every desire

Fear and apprehension on this path, negate oneness
*   and drive you to polytheism*
Thus distancing you away from cognitive certitude
They possess not stability

32. Mawlānā Jalāl al-Dīn Rūmī, *Mathnawī*: IV, 1407.

The vertex of an angle merges into one point
The two sides from that point do originate
By mutual repellence[33] in their ascent

O pure hearted! This is the hidden polytheism
Pull your self out of this abyss
Emerge out of the fetus state

Fantasy will never find the way to perception,
                nor cognition
Leave it and go away! Surely its steps
                are in duration brief
Moreover, fantasy [as one of mind's faculties]
                is not aware of Truth

---

33. The term *tanāfur*, here translated "mutual repellence", is a technical term in Sufi language of discourse. Its signification is not the ordinary meaning associated with its common use, which is "mutual hate." In this technical context it signifies one of two types of cosmic motion, say between "a" and "b": attraction, as "a's" motion towards "b"; repulsion, as the motion "a" away from "b". See for example, Avicenna, *Risāla fī al-ʿIshq*, ed. Mehren (Berlin, 1933).

Your God is the hidden, you unravel and thus behold
The pre-supposed; but never by unveiling seen, is just
   some thing removed from God
Be it a particle that is seen,
    after the atom you have split

The way to God is not traversed by acumen
    nor skillful ruse
The guide on the path to God is none but the Pīr
This cannot be explained

Do not tread this path without a guide
Gabriel's wings were burnt on this path
By the fire of God the Glorious

Out of this spell from which the path has become
  an "up-side-down" labyrinth
Only by following the Path — the Pīr's guidance
Guides the wayfarer to God

"Pīr" here signifies God's mirror and his reflection,
Who is perfect loci for the manifestation
  of divine Essence[34]
All are the proofs of God

If you are not annihilated before the Pīr
Then whoever you may be,
  Satan's path you shall surely follow
Infidelity only thus shall behold your heart

---

34. The technical phenomenological term that best renders the author's intention is "hierophany."

Unless you breakout from Satan's grip
You will not find the straight path
Blind and barren you will remain

Should you be one of the pious,
seeking spiritual growth
The learned Pīr shall then guide you
all the way to God
By witnessing the signs-manifest with proof

Dear One! Men of God are the
Principles of perfection,
They bear no resemblance to irrational thugs
Who feud for worldly goods

He is God's Apostle and governed the soul
And, is the best earthly display of God's Essence
He is a true measure of the good

When, in the station[35] of "Proximity", the prefix
  "not" to "I-ness" annihilates selfhood
Then, capable shall you become to mirror-like reflect
  [the Primal Light]
Your individuation complete, you then shall
  have no one equal unto you

When God's grace surpasses all measure
The figure of the King then shall be yourself
Thereby is attained certainty in faith

35. In Sufism, theories of the soul and the science of psychology commenced during the 8th century C.E. both in the Khūrāsān School and
in the Basra School. The former was radical in its foundations, and
the latter sedate and mainly based on purification through abstinence. However, Sufi psychology developed and in its current form
encompasses an elaborate structure of states, *ahwāl*, and stations,
maqāmāt, of the soul. When the Sufi Master recognizes disorder of
the soul, he will attempt to guide the pupil back to the harmonious
manner the states and stations must function.

The Pīr's pure face is qibla[36] to this world
'Tis he, who in every age, is the keeper
of the Breath's secret
'Tis he who beholds secrets of divine knowledge

He is Noah's Ark, the virtuous Pīr
And knows secrets of the sea
He reveals secrets veiled

Rather, he is both the Ark and the sea
And secret of divine Names
Dot under the letter "ba"[37], is he

36 Direction towards which Muslims face while praying.
37 Reference is made to a saying of Imām ʿAlī. He says that all the
knowledge of the Qurʾān is contained in the *Fātiha* (first *Sūra* of the
Qurʾān); all of which is contained in the *basmallāh* (the salutation that
opens the verse, "In the Name of God"); this in turn is contained in
the "ba"; and "I am the dot under the 'ba'".

His face 'tis key to the door of the Exalted Name
Secrets came under, together all, his magic spell
The entire universe directed towards his face

'Tis the Hand of God that moves and guides him,
From his sleeve, it seems, 'tis His Hand
　　　　　that moves all things
Many intelligent minds struck by awe shall be,
　　　　　when this event they "see"[38]
The seeker yearns for him

Renounce self-hood so your I-ness may become
　　　　　annihilated in Him
You shall become Him,
　　　　　if you do all this solely for Him
His companion you'll be

38. God acting through the corporeal human body is one of the Qurʾān's most cherished signs to countless Sufi Gnostics. For them this signifies the possibility of and opens the door to union with God. For example, "Thou didst not cast [the spears in battle] but it was God who did cast." Qurʾān: VIII, 17

Since you are a limited entity,
the Whole you know not
Deafen ears of your soul from clamors of drums
And from Plato's theory of Forms

How can a particular intellect gain cognizance
of the Universal Intellect
Those ignorant, without vision, cannot be guides
on the Path
Thorns may not be likened to flowers

They often voice pretensions, void of meaning
and authenticity
Amusing? Yes perhaps, watching them perform
their deeds
Be calm! The Perfect Intellect is never blind

In every epoch demon-like "guides" appear anew
To push man astray from the path
with perfidious cunning
Thus to throw man in the Fires of Hell

God says not to eat from this wheat[39]
Do not severe your ties with heart's firm solid rope[40]
Break the chains! Be free!

Whosoever is of Satan's kind, the beast,
Will seek help from his own soul's "Satan"
Seek Satan, he will

He whose soul God's Zephyr has caressed
Then, at every instant he shall see
luminous the soul and heart
And will receive hundred God-given blessings

39. Qurʾān: XXIX, 5.
40. Qurʾān: I, 4.

'Tis not weakness that "faqr"[41] imbibes
Nor are frailty and indigence its goal
Light not for the blind, 'tis meant

Seclusion is to renounce the carnal self
Any hermit unaware is only distraught
Such are the works of fools

If you have strength, then cut off from all desires
Lest the carnal self, your soul should rule
A mouse the lion then, will rule

As long as attachments attract and move you about
Allured by "spiritual retreat"[42] is only deceitful
For there you are bonded still to the body

---

41. *Faqr*, lit. "poverty", is one of Sufism's basic tenets. Cf. The Franciscan notion of "poverty".

42. A common practice in many monastic orders and in structured *tasa-wwuf-i khāneqahi*, monastic Sufism. The praxis usually consists of making pre-set vows to, for example, spend forty days and nights in some secluded monastery; or fast for a period; or read the scriptures for a period interrupted only by human needs and by obligatory acts to God.

Be a man of God among His creatures
Lest, O you! Attracted be to glistening
        garb and gear
Knowing not what the garb manifests in truth

Do not abandon your own inner self true
Leave your self-ness before pure souls; be not tipsy
        like donkeys from too much jaw[43]
Don't join the rank of those debased

You are a soul vast as the universe,
        yet ignorant of it
Kingdom gained without bloodshed and pain,
        'tis what humanity is
Should God be their only guide

43. Jaw is harvested bunches of barley, and when some of its stalks
ferment when stored in damp unlighted places, will cause donkeys
too become "tipsy".

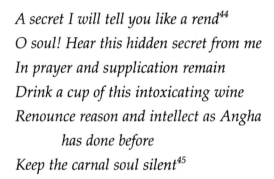

A secret I will tell you like a rend[44]
O soul! Hear this hidden secret from me
In prayer and supplication remain
Drink a cup of this intoxicating wine
Renounce reason and intellect as Angha
        has done before
Keep the carnal soul silent[45]

✧ ✧ ✧ ✧

44. *Rend*, literally means "rogue", "wayfarer", etc. In Sufism *rend* signifies a high-ranking, unusually adept, and gifted teacher-master. The *rend* has gained unity, his outer persona and his inner self are not given to differentiation, nor can they be distinguished.
45. The Persian noun *khamush* (silent, and its derived adjective *khamushi*), have many significations in the present text: 1- reference to Rūmī's *Takhallus*; 2- "silence" in the sense of abandon and retreat from society; and 3- "silence" as in darkness.

He, the Exalted Lord God

Apprehension through the senses is

bound by space extended

Senses are blind when unseen

Knowledge[46] *is sought*

46. "knowledge,"I Arabic *ʿilm*, Persian *danish*, is a technical term in every domain of Islamic intellectual endeavor. Above all the triliteral verb *ʿ-l-m* along with its numerous derivatives both as the 11 most commonly used verbal forms (for example: form II, *bāb tafʿīl*; form III, *bāb mufāʿala*; form IV, *bab ifʿal*, etc.) are the most prevalent terms in the Qurʾān. The following is a basic outline of this subject: 1- The most basic meaning of *ʿilm* is equivalent to the Latin *scientia* — thus, jurisprudence is a science as well as mathematics is a science. 2- The most general division of *ʿilm* is between the transmitted (scripture and oral traditions) sciences, and the intellectual sciences. 3- The intellectual sciences — commonly also known as philosophy, or the science of philosophy — are given an elaborate and comprehensive structure. The following are its basic divisions: a- Theoretical Sciences (or, Philosophy; they are synonymous), which include logic, mathematics, physics, and a two-part metaphysics, and b- Practical Sciences; which

Thus, knowledge gained

of changing flux

Is like the throne whose pillars

sway with the wind

include political philosophy and politics; economics; and mechanics. 4- Gradually the term *ʿilm* was given other significations mainly as variations of the typology of knowledge, and used usually in construct, some of which are: a- *ʿilm-i ghayb*, God's knowledge of the Unseen, which in the Qurʾān it is said to be only God's, but later Sufism employed the epistemology of Knowledge by Presence to prove that select humans may also have knowledge of the Unseen; b- *ʿilm-i ishrāqī*, intuitive knowledge; c- *ʿilm-i mukashifi*, visionary knowledge; d- *ʿilm-i ilhami*, inspired knowledge, and so on. Most of this typology rests on the unified epistemological theory constructed in the 12th century by Suhrawardī (executed, 1191 C.E.) in his novel *Philosophy of Illumination*. The novel holistic system demonstrates that all types of "knowledge" are "scientifically" valid; i.e. they have the same epistemic status as demonstrated knowledge, *ʿilm-i burhānī*. See Hossein Ziai, *Knowledge and Illumination* (Atlanta, 1990).

O you! Tangled in webs of your desire,
How long will you in ignorance move about,
        worthless naught?
Prepare yourself as Adam did

Free your soul of material bondage
Turn to yourself and thus rejoice
        in your heart's selflessness
Throw away all bonds to the wind

Now take on man's trodden path to Truth
Ignorance push aside,
        and remove anguish from your heart
Receive the emanating Grace of God!

Distance yourself, briefly, from the axis of sense[47]
Then take pride and turn away from
        sense-perception
So become seeker of the Light of God
        revealed to Moses on Mt. Sinai

Senses as veils, obscure what your conscience says
Guardians of the veil they are,
        and secrets hidden from you they keep
This is the secret of your ignorance

God's seal on man's soul is the senses
Anyone enslaved by the senses is one devoid of
        value in both worlds
Should "gold" turn black, then "copper" it is

---

47. The five outer senses: sight, sound, taste, smell, and hearing. In Sufism, if one only seeks knowledge by what he can so sense, he will never gain access to the inner, which is not "sensed" by the outer five faculties of sense-perception.

Senses are of equal rank to surfaces and effects
But bound within their own limitations,
      nothing more
So secrets they cannot unveil

Each of the senses have distinct requirements
Which govern varying data they each control
With differing manifestations

Sound is the ear's limit, not the eye
The ear, is "deaf" to all senses not its own
It functions within limits permitted

The nerves of our auditory system
Only detect echoes and sounds
This is their function set

The eye is on the level of colors and light
The eye is "blind" in perceiving sounds
They are beyond its domain

Likewise, each sense's apprehension
Is based upon this law and principle
Analogies may be drawn

To each sense an innate function all its own
An axis away from which it cannot go
Herein lies no alternative

Thus, all things perceived are shaped by your
own senses' reach
Measures of senses are constant not
Thus unstable are all judgments rendered by senses

Being — the One — is not reduced, nor equated
with, four-as-four ones, nor threes
The apparent form, is surely not the being's reality
It's but a fleeting illusion

Water transforms when conditions are changed
At times it turns to ice, and at other times to vapor
Take heed, O alert one

Here, the real principle[48] essence is water
Contraction and expansion are only accidents[49]
Do not reject such rational principles [of reality]

---

48. Substance, essence which is self-existent and self-conscious.
49. Accidents are like attributes of substances, their existence is not self-constituted, but is dependent on the existence of substances.

These accidents cannot exist
    without the substance "water"
All such manifest accidents are names,
    possessing not independent reality
Non-existence does not exist

Therefore, since sense-perception plus their forms
Have effects within the limits of your senses
With countless fluctuations

Upon accepting an elevated level,
    and became the sound and the light
Then the principle wave was covered only
    in appearance
Since it is beyond the limits of sense

As the light's vibration is magnified
And travels beyond the limit of your senses
The eye is thereby deceived

The essence of light will seem darkened to you
That is reason of the weakness of our senses
Seeing nothing but only things materially apparent

Non-existent you thus will name
*   the unique Existence*
And such is the error of your superficial senses
And your warmth will thus turn cold

Should even the senses be armed relative to
*   their own objective*
They still could not go beyond their limits
They are their own confirmations

Our senses are not the measure for realities
       beyond the corporeal
They are not so pure as to apprehend
       realities beyond
Revelation is not similar to perception

Hiding truth is infidelity
Let us transcend rational thought
       and enter realms beyond
Let us turn to silence

The limited will never come to know the unlimited
Although with precision it can split hair from hair
It turned away from the truth

✧ ✧ ✧ ✧

He, the Exalted Lord God

Being is beyond all limitation
of number[50]
'Tis existence as named which "ends"
at limit's bound[51]

50. This point is in reference to a significant and deep theoretical principle regarding the metaphysics of One. Briefly, should we say God is "One" we are limiting Him to human limited knowledge of "one thing," i.e. to a special case of the logical existential quantifier. Or, if we say God is "The First" we still limit Him to human conception of order. So, God is beyond ordinal and cardinal one, beyond unit, etc. The way we may attempt at a more precise attribution of "unicity" to God is to say: God is One from each and every possible modality, now and forever and in all possible worlds. This is simply stated "Absolute One," *wahid-i mutlaq*.

51. Here the analogy is with the series of all natural numbers: they start at "- infinity" and go to "+infinity;" yet most think that one is the starting lower bound.

At every instant, from non-existence to

Existence it leaps

Unending Existence, in the negation of

your being and mine, is.

These realms are all signs[52] of God
Reflections of Absolute Existence they are
And derived from the Truth

The never ending Visage is union's upsurge
When given to rank and states,
      then multiplicity sets in
'Tis the wave of generosity and grace

Ideas[53] are luster of radiating existence
Vacillating — once at the apogee,
      and again at the nadir
Always in the state of intoxication

---

52. Refers to *āyāt* (Qurʾānic verses), each a manifestation and a "sign" (the lit. meaning of *āya*) of God.
53. Ideas, forms, Platonic ideas. Forms represent archetype-like eternal, changeless "ideas" whose existence is both real and independent of the mind. In Suhrawardī's *Philosophy of Illumination* the Platonic ideas/forms (which in Greek philosophy were part of an ideal, limited, and discrete cosmos) are integrated into continuum reality. The cosmos, and all realms of being are "sectors" in the continuum but not disjoint from it.

You chose to delimit Being by a "name"[54]
This caused the addition of contradiction's difficulty
This problem you must resolve

A labyrinth of problems you have created
The Evil and the Good, Light and Darkness
Each the opposite of the other

In the physical world there are four
*   contradictory natures*[55]
But inwardly they are interdependent
And all have the same origin

54. To choose to determine something, i.e., to separate and thus to distinguish it from all else. Sufis, however, (following the early non-Aristotelian philosophers) believed that when something is named then it is limited by it. But since Being is infinite and without limit, to name Being, or Existence, limits it; which in turn leads to contradiction.

55. The four elements of Greek physics: earth, air, fire, and water.

Reality is a continuum whole,

> *so entities are connected not discrete*

So how can there be a tiered path from one to many

In all manifested and existent entities [such is true]

You have given your heart over to your senses

> *to control*

Because of such acts you have strayed from the Path

For just this simple reason

Go, and leave the limitation of senses behind

And then as Sufis do, delve, head first,

> *into the essence of sense*

Go, seek the path that shows you how to

> *prove the senses*[56]

56. This signifies that the novice may reach a spiritual station wherein supra rational as well as deductive methods of the intellect give way to the typology of intuitive cognitive modes. Truths such obtained are not only as valid as the constructed rational, but they are obtained in a temporal and spatially not extended epistemic modes. In common language this is the undoubted certain validity of intuition.

Through the soul one finds the way to the senses
Each instant uncovering the veils from the senses
Nourishing the soul

The Sufi's senses are integrated to his soul
His soul the measure of the senses' knowledge gained
His faith with certitude 'tis

When senses do "remember pre-cognizant"[57] truth
Then freed from attachments
>   *and restrains you shall be*
His limitations so broken

---

57. In Plato's *Theory of Knowledge*, which had a major impact on the development of post-Avicennan Speculative *ʿIrfān* in Iran, "remembering" or "inner recovery of innate things," is the highest form and foundation for epistemological constructivist activity.

As he gazes upon the world's variegate,
colorful, and becoming[58]
His inner soul on the way to unity hastens fast
With love and wisdom far wings

His soul not lost in contradictions is
Yet all others save absolute Essence
have lost His memory
The pillar of His support is not the wind

Who else than the non-composite wave,
though 'tis uncountable
When will his mind take on another type of logic[59]
Without any evidence?

58. Being and becoming are two complementary terms. Here "becoming" signifies eternal creation, and all its states of flux.
59. Reference is made to non-standard, non-Aristotelian logic, which originated in 12th century Iranian Illuminationist philosophy. In this type of logic, many of the classical laws of two-way logic-thought to be immutable — are or may be rejected. The "other" logic is open to phenomena beyond the merely sensed, and validates the intuitive (and other extraordinary and supra sensory) epistemological mode.

There is but one wave and not a multiplicity
Anything at the "bottom's" reef is its own
    highest apogee
The wave is neither even nor odd

This is why sages of years gone by, did thus
    proclaim:
"Relation"[60], does not stand,
    not upon even His essence own
Save yourself from hardship

Thus, darkness is filled with the light of mercy
For, the water of life[61] is hidden in darkness
Unity is within unity

---

60. In Aristotelian philosophy, included in logic, are ten categories, *maqulāt-i dah-gana*, which are to be used to examine a thing. They are: substance, quantity, quality, relation, place, time, posture, state, action, and passion. Here the author draws from Illuminationist philosophy which rejects the ten, reduces them to five (similar to the Stoic 4) and moves them to physics, wherein to be used to "coordinate" the thing studied.
61. Also, "fountain of youth".

Far-ness, proximity, speed, journey, and time
Plus whatever else science and reason proclaim
From space and of its negation[62]

Or, the manifestation of parts
 within the ordered whole
What name does it have on its own?
Hear all this from me

These are terms, senses they signify
And earthly they are, all trapped inside
 the pit hollowed in sand
With recourse to baseless analogies

62 In Sufism *lā-makān* ("non-space") exists and is a type of space; it exists together, and at the same time, with *makān* ("space") within the whole continuum.

Do you know what is "creation-in-time-without
  duration";[63] and what means "pre-eternal?"
Or, what the philosopher-sage has meant by them?
Without doubt, hesitation, nor fear

So that out of contractions and expansions[64]
  of possible existents,
Gradually, the Path leading to Essence
  will before you appear
Where life's secret shall be rendered intelligible

63. This is in reference to: 1- Medieval Iranian-Islamic philosophy, especially to the 17th century creative thinker Mir Damad's theory of creation named *"Hudūth-i Dahrī,"* lit. "Eternal Creation in Time Without Measure"; and 2- Henry Bergson's, *L'Évolution Créatrice* (Paris, 1907), where the concept of *temps sans durée* (durationless time) was developed to explain a special, thought to be "novel," theory of Creation .

64. *Qabz wa bast* are technical terms of Sufism's theory of states and stations of the soul.

Words[65] and rules they govern,
     render any discourse credible
Meanings are the "kernel" and words the
     "covering shell"
To speak of the Good is a good itself

This is the relation between the outer and the inner
Words alone cannot signify the unqualified
     meaning whole
They have many deficiencies

If you do not know meanings signified
     by terms employed
Then, terms alone will not inform you
     the meanings at all
Not in the least bit

---

65. *Lafz*, its technical equivalent is "term". Things, terms, and meanings comprise the main subject of semantic theory here referred.

If ascension's way unto you is closed
Then, your heart will never be acquainted
      with secrets foretold
Your knowledge thus will not be proximate,
      as your wealth

✧ ✧ ✧ ✧

He, the Exalted Lord God

Through the four elements —
water, wind, earth, and fire —
And on the axis of four, five,
seven, nine, and six,
Behold existence's manifestations
And more magnificent yet,
Should your heart be illuminated
Then, steadfast be in your
vow of silence.

While a wave rises and falls
Mirror-like they reflect everyone's essential shape
Tell your cognitive faculty to elevate itself

When the unlimited wave became condensed
It manifested the form of the sensible physical things
Testing its own existence

Each one allocated to a decreed rank
Thus becoming what was determined for him
    in creation
By becoming number, it turned to a countable entity

Contractions and expansions out of vibrations
The different stages of existence were thus manifest
Noble sir[66], do comprehend this

---

66. The Persian suffix -tash — a rare one — connotes "relation with some historical (usually of Altaic origin) clan, or otherwise noble lineage."

Since Existence was at the peak of its perfection
Thus attributes, specific to its creation, all came to be
Non-existence thus existence did manifest

Thus, the one who truthfully acts,
         'tis he a secret of God
God's secrets are Absolute Being's acts
God's Essence cannot be a thing derived

The one who so acts, is no other than
         "secrets of the wave"
And, it appeared to circumscribe, to gather all
         within — the lowest depraved and the high
Be they even, or odd

Out of being, action, and the agent one
Without doubt, the Gnostics intend only one
Reflect on this for awhile

Each and everything, distinguished by rank, is given
         a name different than those of other ranks
Because it is due to obligation that the thing
         "appears" no longer, hidden under
         darkness' veil
Such grace, are but God-given

Since the ranks are themselves not countable[67]
Thus the senses are "blind"
         even to their own essences
Sensing things is not the same as "seeing" them
         in visions[68]

---

67. In these lines, indicative of deep knowledge of essential techniques and truths of many "sciences" a significant concept of contemporary Number Theory is repeated. As here presented, it relates to the epistemology of the One and the many; as well as to the nature of the algorithm: from One to multiplicity. Thus, sense-perception cannot fathom the multiplicity of becoming-essence away from the One source. For sense-perception is identified, in part, as man's faculty to discretely enumerate and likewise bring them together by counting them. This, then is a principle dilemma and limitation of knowledge by sensation. In sum, to know the multiplicity — the whole as continuum — "counting" will fail, rather the Whole may only be known by holistic "visions".

68. See fn. 5.

Any one outer sense-here the subject in sense-
       perception[69] may at best obtain sense-data.
Many a veil cover the essence, thus obscuring it,
       all veils of senses, or their effects
Behold this demonstration revealed

Another sense and mind, not of the common kind
Are necessary to look into being and
       penetrate the essence
Thus to surely truths disclose

Denial is only your self-hardship
Plus proclamations unleashed, inflate your ego
Your idolatry

---

69. The author's principal view of limited sense is more in harmony with the rational Aristotelian and with parts of 20th century analytic philosophy-both reject Platonic realism as well as its subsequent refinement and development.

As long as you are flaunting your senses
'Tis for you, surely, difficult to accept
          what is said of you
Even when the words, and only the words,
          possess formal beauty

Are you a droplet? Submerged? If so, remain
          drowned in Existence's Ocean
Then, tell droplets all to remain submerged, too,
          from head to toe
Take on the locus of the daily eternal rising
          of the sun

As long as you are bound within a pre-determined
place, spatially extended
No drop ever turns into a sea
The drop is limited, alas!
When a drop of the sea of existence, is prefixed with
"not" (lā)[70], it thus will cease to be
And no longer the singular drop, but the sea
When it becomes "not" (lā), it then becomes illā[71]

The drop has no boundary in the deep sea
There's no separation there my friend
Turn from your ways

70. Negating a thing by the use of the prefix "not", being and non-being become "connected".
71. *Illā* is the exceptitive connector in the Muslim article of faith. Its lexicographic meaning is, "except", "save but", "no other", etc. But, in Sufism it signifies yet a higher level of signification; which, when in a state of acting, symbolizes the utter demolition of all-each and every-existent entity by the will of God. Moreover, together with the preceding negating "*lā*", it proves the unicity of God and human willingness to accept only His command, and to thus destroy all idols, including "idols" of the mind.

The sea contains uncountable drops
Water is both the droplet and the sea
Seek the secret of Existence

While the sea, as whole, is all water,
      yet when separated into parts
The particulars are named "drops";
      while the whole, "sea"
It is you, yourself will give away

Ponder how the drops are all contained in the sea
How are you then obliterated within this thing,
      unlimited that-it-is?
Bewildered and obstructed before mere words

In this infinite sea of Existence unbound
You are a tool, and the guardian is pure action
Find this truth in your soul

Existence is God's pure Essence alone
Be as seeker of Essence, to obtain cognizance of God
You who seek God only when you bemoan

❖ ❖ ❖ ❖

He, the Exalted Lord God

From the moon up to the ninth heaven,

'tis the Earth the one selected

No traveler will lose his path

While imbibed in Everlasting Power

We too, are companions: from galaxies

to atoms alike

The potential force in any single object
Changeless 'tis, and extended not
This is agreed upon

Since not related 'tis He to each
          and every other thing
He journeys in His own world thus, but in no other
Any other judgment is incorrect

Neither change nor transformation
Effects, His immutable power, in the least
With thousands of vicissitudes

None better principle axiom this theory has proven
Better even, than the universe whole
All propositions are wanting and irrelevant

Any change or transformation to Him associated
Is a groundless empty word, without any effect
upon His Essence
'Tis He I have proven here

All changes, things becoming other,
and things that do appear
Are all moving through His force
While things moving are material, the force that
moves them is incorporeal light

Matter is composed of energy and power[72]
The energy in matter induces bodily motion
Such is sound science

72. Lit. genus, i.e., material body is like a genus whose "species" include energy and power. In the theory of physics in "matter" there is energy which acts as power and moves things.

A thing accidental is what differentiates
      between the two
Otherwise, no difference will there be between
      matter and energy
If difference is a principle, then what is it?

Thus, forms and things are not the reality
      they appear
No one takes accidents to be causes of things
Guardian is their Primary principles

Principles of [science] do not change
Principles are not given to states of flux,
      and do not move
None exists but Him

Know that movements directed to satisfy needs
Principles have no "need", thus do not move
      through a "mover"
Thus, upon no journey shall they embark

The principle of Being itself is proof for such inner
      meanings we have discussed
Principle of Being was self-constituted
      ever since pre-eternity
Both in realms unseen and seen

The cause is evident in the effect
Since effects are established by the cause
Know the two to be one

By self-as-self, that is, [in notable cases],
        without any cause
An exigency may befall upon certain states
When even no power has been a constituent
        of it occurring at all

Such statements are devoid of logical foundations
        and false are they
This is because all things move by design;
        a need [to achieve perfection][73]
Understanding its signification is easy

Within the principle of Being there is a self-sign
Yet, therein words have no place
Do see who the stranger is there

---

73. All are directed (by cosmic order, or by conscious choice) to an "end". This "end" (*telos* in Greek, and *nihāya* its Arabic equivalent) is Absolute Perfection (which is good and divine). This movement from imperfection to perfection and ultimately a "journey", as a means to attain the Absolute (good/perfection, etc.) is known as "Teleological Movement" — i.e. directed motion toward a final terminus, the *Telos* of life.

Being is infinite there
Freed of all boundary, 'tis absolved of limitations
Unlimited Being alone is the dignity of God

Yet your argument is limited by the inherent
      limits of speech
Cause and effect was thus generated
Such manifest that no boundaries encompass it

Anything exigent has a cause
And is slave to conditions and states pre-determined
The extent of its resolve shall count [to resolve this]

Should mechanical work be your allegory
It will never count as a legally valid demonstration
This allegory is weak [though it may unravel
      who you are]

Anyone knowledgeable without hesitation knows
That, in all things moving there is the One
        who moves them all
The wheel does turn

Who is the source of the master's knowledge?
By whom discoveries in the world were inspired
Who reveals to you the Unseen

If knowledge of the discoverer be taken away
        from the discovery
Then nothing but vain words remain
All empty uttered sounds

Machine is shaped by knowledge
Here lies knowledge's triumphal legacy
Observe the effect of knowledge

Knowledge without form is absolute existence
Yet, formless knowledge an empty thing
*   without a core*
Don't be trapped by this [mystifying] concept

Knowledge without form, which the soul
*   reveals to us*
'Tis the underlying form, given shape,
*   you must seek*
Its embodiment is man

As it seeks to descend away from abstraction along
*   the arch of descent*
In each and every one of its states of being, a new
*   existent entity with a distinct form,*
*   will ensue forth*
Unravel what this statement signifies more deeply

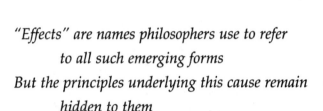

"Effects" are names philosophers use to refer
to all such emerging forms
But the principles underlying this cause remain
hidden to them
The thing is therefore distinguished from union

By "forms" I do not intend the categories
"quality" or "quantity"
Because judgments pertaining to
non-being from them do ensue
Changes form all the time

My intention is essence's ultimate capacity
Where non-existence has no part
For existence is its very foundation

✧ ✧ ✧ ✧

He, the Exalted Lord God

'Til your selfhood is still existent
You are but an idolater, and
Inebriated from the wine of ignorance
You are nothing; and even less
'Til your selfhood remains
Do you know who you are?
When you are freed from selfhood, then
You are all.

Law is measured[74] by purified human senses
Otherwise, nature's principles are measureless
Truly, what is measure?

We cannot measure Existence by
 limited canons humans wrote
The limitless can never be measured, nor counted,
 in any way[75]
Otherwise, problems arise

Senses can never access things bodily, those bound
 by the three dimensions
Thus their reach is limited by coordinated space
They confound the mind

74. The term *bu'd* has several levels of semantic significations. The most common is "spatial dimension" (i.e., length, breadth, depth). Next it signifies "farness" in both physical and non-corporeal space (this level is opposite to "proximity" explained above).
75. This is a reference to foundations of mathematical number theory. "Limitless" is the equivalent of "potential infinity" (as opposed to "actual infinity" proven invalid, or impossible to exist) as first described by Aristotle.

Whoever saw a thing this much long, that much
        wide, and so deep, at the path's end
Indeed, he is slave to the senses
Trapped, in the web of the senses

Slave of senses, like a child, yet with no discernment
Lovingly attracted to raisins and nuts is he
Lovingly plays with worthless coins

Know you where the infinity's center is situated?
From the atom's nucleus to infinity
Wherever you look, there is God

Such meaning as this signifies not a limited goal
My singular most specific desire, yet,
        is nothing but this goal
It's God's command

In the machination of Creation
*   there is not a single imperfection*
It is man's senses, limited that they are,
*   which perceive defects*
He has accepted to live within the limited

Colors proved existence of intricate shapes
Thus all "seen"[76] entities were made "symbols"
*   of "Essence" by Him*
And all Signs this very [principle of being]
*   they do depict*

When a shadow claims to be a real object
The child's eye will accept its claim
Since the child does not know right from wrong

76. The technical term used here, *ta'ayyun*, signifying (at this level) "bestowing a thing with the attribute *Evidenz*." The German term *Evidenz* is used here because the English term "evident" does not indicate this level of semantic signification. It is the *Evidenz*, or *Zuhūr* in a thing that makes it possible for the knowing subject to "see" it, and to thus know it. All this occurs in a "duration-less time."

The form in its gradation of shadows
Manifests the being in non-existence
With manifestations each instant

Non-existence took on shape, thus Existence
"appeared"[77] and was "seen"[78]
And thus mirror-like reflect the Light of God
Our eyes thus were stunned, and we give in to awe

It took on shape-as light and form
So that the secrets of existence would not be divulged
Did you hear the secret from the tree[79]

77. See fn. 5.
78. See fn. 5.
79. "Tree" (*shajara*) is a Qurʾānic term occurring in 18 *āyas*, mostly in the Biblical sense. But also qualified with attributes such as "auspicious" (*mubāraka* — XXIV, 35), "good" (*tayyiba* — XIV, 24). In this verse, however, reference is made to two complimentary ideas: 1- The sanctified tree of the genealogy of the sin-less *Shīʿite Imāms*; and 2- The genealogical tree of a Sufi *tarīqa*, listing all *Pīrs*, and in this case the "Tree" includes the 1st century A.H. Uways al-Qarani.

*If you sweep away all such false images from
         existence's face
Then no longer a lie: All claimants will surely be
         identified in every place
All things are cast from His shadow*

*Ponder this: All images shaped are play things
         in non-existent's hand
And see how at every moment they boast of
         this or that
The cause of sorrow and joy*

*Each boasting of its own being
The image pure, yet bragging pretension
Fabricating colors and forms*

Colors have no definite boundaries
Though each is described by a name
Even if you don't admit it

Look at all colors within the spectrum
You shall see no limit, look with great care
They are all colors and images given form

The universe in essence is colorless[80]
From which the senses perceive hundred colors
Through proportion, or comparison

The secret of "He is more Knowing than Thee"[81]
    in pre-eternity
Is nothing but "[We take] color from God";[82] *O Sir!*
The result is one who seeks gnosis

80. Another way the author makes an attempt to explicate the idea "limit-less."
81. Qurʾān: LIII, 32
82. Qurʾān: II, 138

Without God's Grace and His Command
Not a single atom will move from its resting place
'Tis in truth a veritable guide

O youth! God willing learn from the illā[83]
Refers to the motion of whatever exists
Read this in the verses

"It is but thy trial of us."[84] *O you, is burdensome*
And 'tis proof of true predestination
Say: "He is God The One."[85]

Who other than God "expandeth his heart . . . [or]
   . . . maketh it narrow"[86]
Who is the True Guide, O sinner! Other than God.
Upon all other than He[87]

83. See fn. 71.
84. Qurʾān: VII, 155
85. Qurʾān: CXII, 1; the first *āya* of one of the most recited verses, and part of the Muslim obligatory daily prayer.
86. Qurʾān: VI, 125.

What is predestination? An essence unchanging
beyond the Good and the Bad
Which so did not contradict God's Choice
See the world's and your own state

Each and every particular being in the world of
Generation and Corruption[88]
Gave its own choice up to God
Since you will obtain what you desire

Should he be with no choice, or with it
Know his predestiny to be the same as his choice
In all of the coming and passing away cosmos

87. *Kullu mā siwā*, is not an exactly worded Qurᵓānic *āya*, but very much in the spirit of many verses indicative of the intended meaning here.
88. Title on one of Aristotle's works on the principles of cosmic physics. Translated into Arabic as *al-kawn wa al-fasād*, it now stands for the changing universe.

There is nothing generated in time in
    Absolute Being
One such that 'twas not and then came to be
There is no "symbol" other than non-being

I said: "This Being is Absolute Perfection."
That which you behold in its appointed place is true
There is no untruth in this statement

"Your space" means: go tend yourself
If you seek God do not turn away from your self
Do differentiate spirit from clay

All things other than you for you are invalid
For all things are beyond your reach but you
See how the Truth fashioned a design

Should you look upon any other than your self
All things other than God will have
        lost their path unto you
Distinguish this from mere admonition

Should you descend from your own lofty place
Truly you have then fallen from the Truth
This is from the standpoint of Intellect

Whatever is other than you is invalid
You are the Truth, in you "thou-ness"
        is the heart's secret
"Heart" is not the body, fashioned from water
        and earth

Reality with referent outside the mind is the
       Truth in any Station
What is Reality other than the sameness of the
       "name" and the "signified."
From soul to clay, throughout

Open your ear! Listen to this choice demonstrated
       unique point
That: "True statements are those said and proven."
Without any fault, nor deficiency

It has been transmitted in Divine Traditions that:
"I am your secret and you mine."[89]
"I" without body and garb!

---

89. "Divine Traditions," *Aḥādīth Qudsī*, are few in number, and of those a small portion are believed to be authentic. They are distinguished from regular Prophetic *Hadīth*, manyfold in number. In the former God speaks, while in the latter God has revealed truths through the archangel Gabriel to the Prophet Muḥammad, who is the speaker, i.e. the subject of the statement.

"Humankind My secret, and I its"[90]
"Humankind is the chalice and I in it."[91]
He is a reed flute and you the same, but lesser

✧ ✧ ✧ ✧

90 Another example of a Divine Tradition.
91 Ibid.

He, the Exalted Lord God

We are the ones who consumed many a

cup of Wine

We have set fire to our selves

Aided by the power of love, and our

Pīr's *firm resolve*

We've abandoned the love of both

worlds in a single instant.

Know, that self-perfection is the highest Empyrean
    of all things
Know, also that the divine high place
    is a Dervish's[92] *heart*
Faqr[93] *is more than this*

Tear veils upon veils covering the "inner" of every
    possible existent.[94]
Thus seek union with the ultimate cause of Essence
In manifestations and in attributes

---

92. *Dervish* is the Persian term used as the equivalent of the Arabic Sufi. However, the term *Dervish* has wider application than Sufi. At the present "Sufi" is an individual who has been initiated into an established *tarīqa*, and has vowed to give total obedience to its Master, uphold the Rules of Conduct (*Ādāb al-Murīdīn*, which varies among the numerous *tarīqas* from northwest China to northern Africa and now to the U.S.) of the Order and be earnest in his/her resolve to take on the vicissitudes of the spiritual journey ahead, guided by the Order's Master. The prevalent meaning in Middle Persian usage of the term is "disciple."
93. See fn. 41.
94. "possible existent," or "possible being," is one of the three modalities: necessity, possibility, and impossibility, which were first fully incorporated into metaphysical scientific thought by the great Persian master philosopher Avicenna in the late 10th century.

The spirit is Revelation and Cause
     creator of Heaven
And, it runs through the core, all the way to
     the certainty of Truth
See the world of the Gnostic

Revelation turns the mineral into plant
And, animals become existent from plants
In the total possible existent entities

In man animal instinct is strong
And, man's soul, drawn by the most attracting love
Open wide this book

Proximity to God is the faithful soul's ascent
     to the heavens
The faithful soul is aware of God's secrets
'Tis he proclaiming revealed words of God

'Til your carnal soul remains satanic and powerful
How can you ever turn towards spiritual love
Which is brought forth by the Truth

Until you're unaware of the secrets of love,
Barren you remain, as thorns without fruit
Being not relentless in all the realms

Where are the ineffable secrets found in you
Where are your signs of longing and madness
In worlds that continue

Forlorn and unmindful, you're not
And, when in such destitute state, the elevated
        mystical experience you seek not
God has no place in you

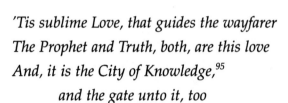

'Tis sublime Love, that guides the wayfarer
The Prophet and Truth, both, are this love
And, it is the City of Knowledge,[95]
>and the gate unto it, too

The lover thinks not of worldly things,
>more, nor less of them
The "Clear Tablet" of his mind is clear and pure
The discoverer of the mystery of eternity

Self-sacrifice is his life's offerings
Madness and drunkenness,
>are his demonstrative ways
Love's warmth is the wares of his store

---

95. Reference to famous and commonly known and accepted as valid
Hadīth: "I am the City of Knowledge and ʿAlī its Gate."

Love's flame his soul has set afire
From the Master of Love, annihilation he's learned
The world, He has illuminated

Faith nor infidelity are not constituents of love's
       ways on the Path
Before love, mosque and tavern are not
       distinguished
Who can endure love's pain

Sanctification to the Path is what is undertaken
       by men pure of heart
Giving up one's self on the Path to love is difficult
Yet, such is the very first stage of progress
       on the Path

Once more Love's consuming fire fell upon the heart
Love for the Pīr took away all my perseverance
It is only love that matters

My soul is tired from all this ritual and bondage
Once again love has stolen my awareness
Testing the Intellect's prowess

Since love's call comes from the heart
So tear away all bonds, as Majnūn[96] did
Pass through the ordeal of love once and
        leave this water and mud

96. Majnūn is the name of the male protagonist in one of the earliest romantic epic stories in history, "The Story of Laylī and Majnūn." Later a genre emerged, which in European literature includes Romeo and Juliet, and Tristan and Isolt.

Once again my heart drags me towards Love
To the path of longing it takes me
It takes me to the depths of secrets

My state of madness became more disheveled
Alas! My state and my legend
My cup, my wine

Love kindled a fire in our soul
Love burned away all selfhood away from me
Love alone taught the soul

Time for the triumph of love did arrive
Majnūn's soul consumed in Laylī's[97] love
Until only love remaind

97. Name of the female protagonist in the romantic epic Laylī and
Majnūn.

We burnt and obliterated our soul for a "vision" of
the Friend[98]
This is how we learned love's secrets
And, we set this life ablaze

Just as the candle, I have risen, then burnt in fire
So that I may also burn all over
And thus to attain complete annihilation

I do not fear not-being, should love exist
Gold is pure if in fire 'tis purged
The heavenly does not originate on earth

We are the manifestation of Love, from head to toe
We are truly Love's prophet
Chivalrous warriors of Love, are we

98. "Friend" is one of the terms in the technical language of Sufi discourse and signifies God.

Madness became keeper of the rein around my
      drunken heart
It is thus that the scent of blood emits from
      what I say
'Tis madness' tune he then played

Love carelessly reveals delicate points and signs,
      without constraint
And so steals my last bit of choice
That is when the beloved becomes inebriated

Our cup and desire's fulfillment overflows with love
Thus we broke all restrictions and became free
The pearl emerged from the shell

Alone, we pillaged blasphemy and faith alike
With conviction and faith we lost the soul
      and the heart
We finished all affairs of the cosmos

We are this as "straw," yet His mountain-full of
      love 'tis for us to carry
Thus, our duty is to unearth the mountain
      with our eye-lashes
Our companions are only the Intellects[99]

I no longer have the impetus to speak
This is so, since you are not fit to know the
      levels of meaning
Your understanding now, pertains to a different
      level of discourse

---

99. "Intellects," are the separate non-corporeal intermediary cosmic beings, including celestial motion.

Let us pass away from this discourse once more
'Tis now time for you to open your ears
and hear other secrets
All connected with domains signified in times past

He, the Exalted Lord God

I am, and in the infinite, I am
The mirror of divine
manifestations, I am
I am the sun, yet hidden inside
an atom, I am
As the Water of Life, in darkness I am

The fifth dimension is your soul's expansion
And 'tis translucent and aware of the "First"[100]
Should your heart seek this secret

Soul seeks to apprehend Being, how can it-wit
mere senses?
Base the search wholly on corporeal analogy
Keep vigil and watch over your soul

[Being is] time-less, space-less, and there are no
intermediate [principle]
Being's time, though, is related to Time
He has no comparable measure

100. *al-Awwal*, in theoretical Sufism, as well as in other religious and mystical interpretations is equated with the archangel of Revelation, i.e. Gabriel. And, it is the medium through which God "speaks" and reveals knowledge to his chosen Messengers and Prophets. Here "awareness", at times said to be obtained by "seeing," or by "vision," is the act that triggers the movement "becoming".

Timeless-ness and space-less-ness are worthy of
    Him [alone]
"Image-less mirror" here signifies His Essence
I have no argument on this issue

He commands Existence beyond all being
Which is why humanity calls it "Universal Soul"
Even though manifestations appear, yet do not last

Should the Soul, O possessor of art![101] Be abstracted
    from all corporeality
He shall not be limited to any of the [Aristotelian]
    categories, quantity and quality
He is beyond quantity, not given to
    "more" nor "less"

---

101. One proficient in technique of the Arts.

And should it wear "intermediary"[102] clothes
Still it shall manifest and radiate with a hundred
colors and shapes
Surely, then it shall be "seen"

The soul cannot be changed nor transformed
It will remain eternal but will take on
variegated manifestations
When it unveils its Face

The pure breath is the Essence indeed,
Go ask this pure one the secrets of life
Everywhere in the generated cosmos

102. The term, *barzakhī*, is a reference to an intermediary realm between Soul and Body. In post Avicennan philosophy this realm is given other designations as well, for example: The Realm of Forms — similar to, but not the same as Plato's Realm Of Ideas, *Mundus Imaginalis*, and The World of Intermediary Being.

"Go become stripped of body, then "see"
the non-material body
This is the condition of "seeing" everything"
Go seek the Truth of knowledge which is attributed
"certitude"[103]

Pass the limits of time and space
Then in God's Realm, you will attain [the Station]
Self-less-ness[104]
One must become the "inner essence of the soul"[105]

103. In the current language of Iranian philosophical thought, signification of the terms: *haqq al-yaqīn* (used in this line), is knowledge, especially of the nouminous. It is obtained through the discursive and the intuitive together, but with an emphasis on the experiential intuitive, with certitude equaling that of the deductive, i.e., demonstrative knowledge. *ʿIlm al-yaqīn*, is knowledge that places the emphasis on the deductive, i.e. syllogistic demonstrative knowledge, which is also certitude knowledge.

104. *Mahw*, means wiped out: from, "a person killed" to "a spot cleaned". But in its technical signification it stands for one of the highest Sufi states and stations wherein the personal identity, "I-ness", and "selfhood-as ego" is no longer, and in its place the personal Identity shares the revered state of "self-less-ness."

*Do not seek the soul in ordinary time/space
    coordinates[106]*

*Do not seek the soul through physical (bodily)
    demonstration[107]*

*Don't permit your own imaginary perceptions
    take over*

105. Stated simply in the language of modern Freudian psychology: this means Identity but without ego, id, nor libido. But in Sufism without them — "identity" or "Self-consciousness" — higher awareness of the person's dynamics of his/her soul not only remains, but is elevated, or more finally analyzed and 'tuned'.

106. "Ordinary time/space" is the ordinary Euclidean, which holds time only at low (or, no) motion. Things coordinated there, are limited to the material extension of such a space, which could be object to any sense-data, limited by our sensing it.

107. Time/space continuum has been proven (1) without Euclidean imposed limits; (2) is completely distorted and incapable of describing holistic Reality (all time, all speed, etc.).

The distance between two points[108] is traveled not
Rather, as "transubstantial motion"[109];
    i.e., as a non-bodily "journey"
Should you fathom this level meaning

One may journey with "capacity" to perfection
'Tis the meaning of past, present and future —
    the undying states of being
Where can you find a place that does not perish

108. Here is a clear reference to only Euclidean Geometry — one of the five postulates since the 19th century through works by: Gauss, Rieman, and others. The real existence of "other" systems of geometry (with imposed limits of Euclidean); where, among other things: (1) the (shortest) distance between two points is not necessarily a straight line; (2) there may be an infinite number of lines drawn from a single point parallel to another line. These revelatory new theories of geometry (which have been known in part in Iran for a 1000 years) may describe: (1) much more inclusive range of the Real; (2) time/space is not the sole measure of time as "measure of distance". It is much more sophisticated.

109. "Trans substantial motion"; also translated "motion-in-category-substance", and also "substantial motion" is a "Theory" — well-constructed and defined — of a Universal Principle ("Universal Constant" in Western scientific terminology) by Sadr al-Dīn Shirāzī, best known as "Mulla Sadra" (17th century) within his holistic "New" system of Scientific Metaphysics (*Hikmat-i Mutaʿāliyā*).

Therefore, "Time" is the attributive description of
His Place and His State [of Being]
And, these accidents are measures of His rapture
They are His divination, which penetrate
*   and are valid*

Without space, time will not exist
Till there is no space, time will not be existent
Though it will be limited only

Since Creation is not a constituent of this meaning
'Twas by the Command "Be",[110] that being appeared,
*   thus existents came to be*
Unveiled His Visage

---

110. Qur'ānic reference to God's creation, "Glory be to Him!" When He simply decreed being and so Created, for example: "Be, and it is." (19: 35) "For to anything which We have willed, We but Command: "Be!', and it is." (16: 40).

The Principle of Creation has no
"beginning nor end."[111]
Where can you see "separation"[112] *among the created*
[entities]: disjunction, connection,
nor points [as bounds]?
What is conjunction, and disjunction,
things created?

111. Creation without beginning and without end, per se, is not signified in Qur'ānic language and expression. Such a concept is first
philosophical and second one developed centuries later than the
Islamic Revelation in the 7th century, subsequent to the essential
integration of the apogee of Greek philosophy (some aspects of it in
their Greek Peripatetic change form) into Islamic peripateticism by
"The Second Teacher" (after Aristotle, "The First"), the creative
Persian philosopher Al-Farabi, and subsequently much refined and
expanded and augmented by the Persian "Principle Master" (*al-
Shaykh al-Ra'īs*) Avicenna. The closest Qur'ānic idea is said only of
God, not of His Creation, and only once: "God is the First, the Last,
the Evident (outer), and the [Hidden] Inner" (Qur'ān: LVII, 3).
112. Here the term, *fasala*, which in ordinary language means: "measured distance in space", or, "sentimental separation", etc. is used in
its distinctly technical mathematical (best say: philosophy of mathematics) sense of "continuity", or "functions without singularities", or
simply "no singularity"; all of which describe the concept and mathematical (and here metaphysical) expression of "continuous" and
"continuum."

"Beginning" and "end" are human creations
This is because the principle of the Prime Principle
        is without beginning from the beginning.
Even though they be manifest [and evident] in
        thousands of ways

The atom, the Sun, the Galaxies and the Universe
Are surely "names, shapes, and forms" [in human
        expression and discourse]
In principle though they are all one[113]

113. More technically stated: "They share sameness in Principle."

Movement as well as the Mover within the Whole
Are pure energy[114] — their wave-like motion,
    non-composite
Even there be many thousands of "things" between
them

114. This is a more modern expression of the philosophical idea first stated by Aristotle as: "pure potentiality" and attributed of the "Cause of causes," the "Mover of movement," which itself does not. See Aristotle, Metaphysics: Book Lambda.

He, the Exalted Lord God

For a while I thought I was seeking
the path to God
But, I was scrutinizing
"I" and "we" as if
They were markers pointing to the Path
When love arrived and the "I"
and "we" removed
Then, selfhood departed, and
annihilated re-entered,
I sought my "self" everywhere.

The unique pearl of the ocean of perfection
It was the inner intellect, and unending love
Messenger of God, Possessor of Glorious Power

Gnosis personified in the ocean of existence's depth
And was seeking this unique "gem"[115]
Thus caused the Appearance of an entire world

It is the Sixth Dimension in the all encompassing
  Sphere of the Firmament
Which thus forged man superior to the angel
It is both measure and standard

115. The term used here translated "gem," is the Persian *gowhar* in its Arabicised form, *jawhar*. Multiple levels of meaning are signified by it: 1- the most common is "gem"; or, "a uniquely precious stone"; 2- a human's "fundamental" (some would add: God given; or innate) base of, or potential for "identity"; 3- in the technical language of philosophical as well as other intellectual discourse it is equivalent to Aristotle's first time specific use, "substance" (*ousia* in Greek), and commonly used synonymously with the Arabic *dhāt* — which is not a precise use in all intellectual domains. Here the English "gem" is used to convey the poetic metaphor.

It is the locus into which this secret descended and
became the human soul
Up to the time when it soared to the
Heavenly Empyrean
Just at the moment when love gushed forth

The first thing created was light of pure love[116]
Radiating from the divine throne down to what
is the Earth
Do not despair due to this

---

116. The Prophetic *Hadīth* here incorporated into the verse is: "The First Thing God Created Was Light." It is frequently quoted, especially in texts such as Abū Hāmīd Ghazzāli's, *Mishkāt al-Anwār*; Avicenna's, *al-Ishārāt wa al-Tanbīhāt*; Suhrawardī's, *Hikmat al-Ishrāq*; Shams al-Dīn Shahrazūrī's, *Al-Shajara al-Ilāhiyya*; etc., in the philosophical domain. And in texts such as, Hujwīrī's, *Kashf al-Mahjūb*; Abū Tālib Makkī's, *Qūt al-Qulūb*; Muhāsibi's, *Makāsib*; Abū Nasr Sarrāj's, *Kitāb al-Lumaᶜ fī al-Tasawwuf*, etc., in the early formative period of Sufism, also in all *Shīᶜite Tafsīr*, *Hadīth*, etc., compilations. But the main Sunni *Hadīth* compilations do not include this *Hadīth* and others similar in spirit, as not *mutawātir*, nor *musnad bi-dūn inqitāᶜ*, and so on. However, light as cosmic material, as source of Reality, etc., has played an important role in Iranian *Shīᶜism* as well as Sufism.

As love fled from the divine throne of comings
    and goings
It first descended upon the "city of soul"
And the world took on order — a cosmos away
    from chaos

The cosmos became the locus for the triumphal love
Then it gushed forth upon the waves of being
    like a warrior-soul
He was both Noah and the Ark

As love's steed galloped through the Heavens
It turned being's potentiality into actuality
And thus emanation imbibed every existent entity
    and propagated everywhere

Love's glamour spread over the entire cosmos
   [by its quality of attraction][117]
Before it, devoid are existent entities all,
   of the power to attract things
Love possesses the ability to "Manage and
   Regulate"[118] *the cosmos*

Everything [in Cosmic Heavens] He controls,
   from the Pleiades to the stars
Everything everywhere in the dominion of being is
   drunken by His Love
Rather, 'tis He who the Being of being is

117. Love's quality of attraction, *jadhbat al-ᶜishq* in Arabic — in Persian Sufism *jadhbeh* is often used alone, not in construct with ᶜ*Ishq* — is one of the two Primary Principles of cosmic motion: attraction and repulsion. The former between things sharing sameness, and the latter between things opposite. See Aristotle. Metaphysics: IV, 2.
118. The term, *tadbīr*, lit. good, or acute management qualities in its common signification, here signifies the cosmic principle of Regulation and Control. Cf. the Empedoclean notions of: Love and Strife and their role as Cosmic motive forces and of cosmic cycle.

Go locate the alphabet of the lexicon
       [of things named] by glistening Love
And find them in the Book of the "Greater
       Universe"[119]
Should you be wakeful, not asleep

The secret of love and loving are indeed separate
       from any and all of this
"Love is the astrolabe of God's secrets"[120]
He is pain and its remedy, both [at the same time]

---

119. In speculative Iranian *ʿIrfān*, the Whole is divided into: the "Greater Universe" (*ʿālam-i Kabīr*), and the "Smaller Universe" (*ʿālam-i Saghīr*), which signify the macrocosm and the microcosm. Further the micro symbolizes (in some texts) the human, and the macro the physical Universe.

120. A half-line; or, hemstitch (*misraʾ*) by Mawlānā Jalāl al-Dīn Rūmī. The line, however is not included in R.A. Nicholson's edition of the *Mathnawī*, but it is found in at least two other editions: The earlier edition widely used and commonly known as *Mathnawī-yi Kulāli-yi Khāwar*; and the rather extended edition commonly known as *Mathnawī-yi Amīr Kabīr* (Name of the publisher).

Love's instrument [and all its accouterments]
have no color
The lover is not in the business of [seeking] fame
nor debasement
There exists no one equal to him in magnitude

Here even the feathers of Gabriel, ["Giver of
Forms"[121]] to the Intellect, were scorched
And, the Intellect itself burnt from head-to-toe
It burnt all over, from toe-to-head

121. In Islamic philosophy as well as speculative gnosis, Gabriel is used as a symbol for the Active Intellect, which is the tenth Intellect of Peripatetic cosmology. Therein it is also attributed with a principle epistemological act, that of "Giver of Forms", "Giver of Knowledge", and "Giver of Soul" (to the human body). It also acts as the Manager and Controller of all existent entities within the sublunary sphere (the tenth in Ptolomaic astronomy) — the model for the Peripatetic cosmic structure. St. Thomas incorporates this into his magnum opus, *Summa Theologia*. He had studied Latin translations of the works of such giants as Alfarabi and Avicenna; and uses the Latin equivalents: *dator formarum, dator scientias, dator spiritis*.

Unto Love there are a hundred veils
  each woven out of madness
The pain of lovers is "homey"[122] [its origin is
    familiar]
This pain, on the other hand, originates from the
"outside" world

Intellect and madness never befriend
The sparrow will not attain the position of the falcon
Love has no partner

This message was not given those of the other view
that:
"How is it that love is the Prophet's right?"
Love is customer in the shop — wants to
    buy the Truth!

---

122. The Persian term, *khānegī*, here translated "homey" more precisely signifies: something sensed in a most familiar place, or something felt by the action, or words, again of someone most familiar —
"family and intimate friends."

Perchance, Love's rank is beyond these limits
Whoever is with us, and yet utters anything but
"God," is an apostate
Love is Ahmad's[123] *essence*

There are many, who purely and freely give never
wanting in turn, in this World
Yet, who are anonymous, no one even knows
their names
How can a meager straw fathom [vastness of]
the ocean

---

123. Ahmad, the superlative substantive of the noun *hamd*, lit. "praise" — thus Ahmad, lit. is "the most praiseworthy — is one of the names given to the Prophet Muḥammad, as an honorific epithet, but a common one and not of the same rank as his other, lofty titles such as: al-Mustafā, lit. "the Chosen"; or, al-Rasūl, "The Messenger" [of God].

Such group of exalted self-less ones are
  in love with God
And united with Him — Gabrielle's actions, yet,
  never even touched them
Love acts as their guide

They are oblivious of themselves,
  and of strangers, too
They absolved themselves of the intellect, and
  embraced madness
They are the truly intense annihilated ones

They feel cramped by the triumphal intellect
Beyond and around the seventh heaven their souls
  have ascended
They are, as Noah, the World's Pole[124]

124. *Qutb-i Ālam*, lit. "World's Pole" is a technical term, described at length by Aziz al-Dīn Nasafī in his Persian didactic text, *Kitāb al-Insān al-Kāmil*, where he presents the view that in each era select humans with extraordinary capabilities exist, and act in a pivotal manner to keep chaos at bay so to allow cosmos its ordered motion.

As when the basmallah[125] *is said, beasts*
    [fearfully] flee
And freed of thoughts, good and bad, they become
At once, and in all, they become freed of any limit

Then they settle in the Empyrean constructed out of
    inner meanings
They become oblivious to "destiny" and
    ramble not of "free will"
They then come to reside in the Station of awe, and
    remain mesmerized beholding
    the Beloved's Face

125. "In the Name of God the Merciful, the Compassionate" is the Sacred Revealed statement (some would prefer, "formula"), which every believer must utter before/at the moment of taking on any task. It is also shortened to (not widely used) *basmallah.* Its use is numerous, here are a few examples: 1- Heading of every one of the 114 Qurʾānic *Sūrat*; 2- Many times in the 17 *rak'at* of the daily five-time obligatory Muslim prayer; 3- At the time of commencement of each and every event of the daily life of a Muslim-for example: starting a meal, entering any place, one's home, a friend's home, etc., and especially when entering sacred places. In sum, every

Their bodies born, just as flowers, from the earth
Their souls elevated beyond the seventh sphere
This is the meaning of Certain Truth

In the Qurʾān's [language]-innermost meaning is
    [hidden] beneath layer upon layers of veils —
Yet, the nucleus' inner core encompasses
    many particles, each one radiating as a Sun
Pages upon pages, as in a book

God''s Essence induces awe in each and every being
Then, what is left of them are merely names
Absorbed in God they are — the Pure, the Exalted

Muslim/Muslima recites (usually audible, though not loud) the *bas-mallah* — certainly at the beginning, but also in its duration — of each and every act (both physical, such as going on a trip, as well as spiritual, such as prayer, divination, etc.) of the daily life — both mundane and sacred.

And, even those [names] become existent due to [the
propagation] of "light" from the [Source]:
the Absolute Essence
You'll see as you ponder, that their names
are those of God
All this, and more, are all due to prior-most
emanation

If you still are puzzled, [nay overtaken], by doubts
concerning the meanings [here signified
through terms]
Then know that "Love, the lover, and the Beloved"
are one.[126]
And, neither is separated from the Real

---

126. The "oneness", "sameness", "identity", "equality", etc. — here
stated in the language of speculative *'irfān* — between the "lover"
(subject), "beloved" (object) with "love" as "relation" (or, "medium";
or, "attribute" of continuum reality), is the author's poetic creative,
albeit being condensed into just one of the two hemistichs of a line —
one element of the set complex of Classical Persian poetic form-an
indication to one of philosophy's most significant and lasting problems.

As long as your heart's mirror is not polished clear
Love for you is nothing but the utterance l-o-v-e
Surely at [this level of understanding] you
      will not fathom the attributes' signification

He, the Exalted Lord God

No separation there shall ever be

between you and God

But, should you never have

apprehended this luminous truth

Then, should you be, or not, obedient

to serve [His Commands]

God will never act Godly once.

The intermediary realms are but ranked
       and ordered being
They became Apparent in an order determined by
       their capabilities
Each one at a stage on the arch of ascent

His inclination [to move along a way] was
       determined, and his attraction to Perfection,
       that which moved him[127]
Drowned were all in the endless ocean
And, in time [all would] perish

He is not given to "infinite regression"[128]
There can never be potential refuge for a thing in act
His actualized Existence is not in Him
       [prior to His Being]

127. "Inclination" to move; and "attraction" are two cosmic principles of motion.
128. "Infinite Regression," here the term, *sayr-i qahqarāʾī*, is proven false in many ways since Aristotle's first clear proof. The earlier proofs, not in notation, are rather simplistic statements and center on

Thus, reincarnation is not a valid principle
How can the soul once more return to the body?
So as to become more purified?

The stages are without limit; they cannot be counted
Just as the numberless bubbles that
> *arise on water's surface*
From where do bubbles come? Water, you'd say

two main ideas: a- The impossibility of any sequence without a terminus (upper bound) — cause and effect, mover and moved, the generation of multiplicity from one, the sequence of integers, of even number, of odd number, as well as all sequences of numbers whose nth term (as an Algorithm) is known (2n; 2nn, etc.). The ancients singled out the sequence of Prime Numbers as a good example of an invalid sequence; b- "Circularity," in any constructed argument is false because it has no limit — it is a fallacy also named, *petitio principi, musādʿada ʿan al-matlūb al-awwal.*

Ranks are many, and structured according to
capability and disposition —
He shall traverse [beyond] dimension in the
"Intermediary Realm,"[129]*; through a*
"perimeter" whose boundary [is not seen]
[This is so] since existence is generous

"Dimensions" in the Realm of Intermediary Being
are measures of "we" and "you"
You and I "appear" to be two in this Realm.
At times [appearing] old, and at times new

129. The realm of Intermediary Being — a sector of/in the Whole
Continuum — is (it has to be repeated) one of the many types of
space, but decidedly non-Euclidean. And, as any "space" it has the
attributes human superficial common sense associates with Euclidean space, however, essentially different.

All such duality will remain existent,
*   until we become one*
You and I, when removed of "I and you,")
*   shall become Him*
And, we shall transfigure into "There is nothing
*   but huwa."[130]*

Union with that Essence, is our origin
Shall purify you and I — remove the intermediary
*   boundaries*
The terminus became just as the origin

---

130. In the above expression *"laysā illā huwa"* (Nothing exists save "He") — when the Arabic third person masculine pronoun, *huwa*, is translated gender-specific; or more precisely, the Law of Contradiction here proves the existence of the third person pronoun, in the Persian usage "It" — the Third Person genderless Persian is *ū*, and the Persian pronunciation of the Arabic *huwa* is *hova*, and might be interpreted as the Persian way to semantically equate *ū* and *huwa*. In the Arabic expression here of, verse 335, L. 3, *"laysā illā huwa,"* the third person Arabic *huwa*, "he," is always pronounced *hova* in Persian (prose and poetry). See fn. 1.

Limitations will there break from all sides
Nothing will remain but the First
To know this suffices

Look with inner eyes, O artful one!
And behold: "He bestows life upon you,
to Him you shall return."[131]
What has been your chosen guide

"You were dead, He gave you life"
He speaks of two deaths and of two lives
Seek its meaning by the Intellect

---

131. The term used in this instance to signify cosmic continuity; i.e. the Whole as Continuum, is the Persian abstract substantive, *jodāʾī*. Earlier, the author's position on cosmic continuity and the Reality is a Continuum was discussed. There the Arabic term, *fāsila*, was employed to convey the concept. Other synonymous technical terms are: the Arabic, *ittisāl*; the Persian noun, *peyvasteh*, and its abstraction, *peyvastegī*; plus the Persian constructed term, *peyvastān*, as equivalent to the idea and reality signified by the English term, "continuum" — usually said of: sets, groups, complexes, and collectivities, whose members (constituents) may be extremely large in number, but countable. This principle Illuminist view posits that all things propagated (distinct from the Peripatetic idea and expression of Emanation).

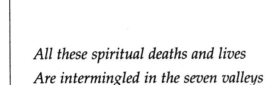

All these spiritual deaths and lives
Are intermingled in the seven valleys
All attesting God's presence

Such is this the journey — the ascension — to God
In ignorance you're dead, change your way
See God before you, in the crust and the core

Become the "Day"[132] *itself, before it arrives*
As resurrection is itself the proof of resurrection
On that day the Trumpet shall sound

Your saying: "Wait, resurrection will come a day;
      in some tomorrow"
Will truly prevent you of true judgment. Alas!
What a pity, this is your deception

132. *Rūz-i alast*, see fn. 25, 136.

Make a complete solar circle
So that resurrection will be shown to you
This is what the day of resurrection is

Recite the verse: "Men die according to how they
have lived"
Such is the state of your death, with
Judgment Day's place — where the
resurrected gather

What is death? That which took away your soul
And, what your soul presented — all it had done
It demanded the true, and not the false

You! Unaware of death: This is your type of rising
    from the dead
Be aware of death, you who are barren
So that you are not left behind the circle

And that absolute eternal resurrection
Listen to the Qurʾānic verse: "We are from God and
    to Him we return."[133]
From the truth and from within

These gone, and those to come are
    non-existent and "lā"
So do heed the "new" if you seek "permanence"[134]
Heed not the passing daily events

---

133. Qurʾān: II, 156.
134. *Baqāʾ*, is the highest Station in the soul's progress. Upon undergoing *fanā*, annihilation and permanence will set within the inner-self, and thus freedom from any and all bondage.

In truth, the whole of Being is a moment
And the secrets of the "moment" is cosmos evident
And, Adam is the mystery of the cosmos

One truth is the "breath's"[135] *secret of secrets*
And that is the presence of the exalted
Who is sempiternal (antecedent from eternity)

The whole world is subject to death and life
Is it but the motion of waves
Who sets the waves to motion

The sum of affirmations and negations
Positive and negative is death and life
If you're only concerned with attributes

---

135. Reference to the numerous Qurʾānic verses where God's Breath is attributed with variegated qualities and powers, especially in construct with "Grace" thus "His Graceful Breath." Place for two examples: VI, 12; & VI, 54.

All outcomes of such transfers as these
Are, descriptions of waves and of their attributes
For example, I did explain this to you

Science is not preoccupied with concepts as these
And I'm not concerned with the physical wave
Though not difficult to explain are they

Yet, since to understand God
You choose to use the mind
Then, yes! Should you be worthy

Out of necessity, words must be brief
That the real path be shown to you
The mountain heap of [outer] meaning,
*   became weight-less straw*

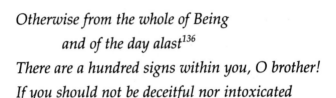

Otherwise from the whole of Being
     and of the day alast[136]
There are a hundred signs within you, O brother!
If you should not be deceitful nor intoxicated

"Those who strive on our path,"[137] is God's
Revelation to His Prophet, for this purpose
If you are searching

136. *a last* and *rūz-e alast* are Qurʾānic terms related to the concept of eternal "covenant" between man and God. The most widely and frequently quoted verse is, "*a lastu bi-rabbikum*" (Qurʾān, 7:71, "Am I not thy Lord?"). In Sufism this becomes a very special idea on the Day of Covenant. Subject of numerous treatises, and well integrated into the meta language of Persian poetic discourse, *rūz-e alast*, with variations, but all in strict conformity with the Qurʾānic dictum when God finds only His desire in the very acceptance of an eternal Covenant; with man accepting to obey God's Covenant — *amr* Allah —: "Am I not thy Lord?" [*a lastu bi-rabbikum* have alast as the main semantic sign]. The literal meaning of the verse, "Am I not thy Lord? Yes! Soundly said all humans", has been given many levels of meaning/semantic signification.
137. God often Commands humankind to obey, lest they burn in Hell, in the Scripture as well as in the Oral Traditions.

To show you what's wrong and what's right
To find the way into your aware heart
To find the right path

If you do accept, then know that it is "I" —
  the Great Name
And, it is that "I" which is in every heart,
  that light within
Luminous, as "They said yes"

Aside from "I", nothing is constant in you
Look within yourself, if you can distinguish
So that as I you may also know

The intermediary, between the higher and the lower,
  is "I"
Allow for cogitation to break up the words
My intention by the use "I", is not the
  signification "body"

That which is unique to you, and remains constant
in you for a lifetime
Does continue long, when the body turns cold
And goes to the Intermediary Realm of Being
[barzakh]

The Principal, simple, and unique substance
of the soul
Does and will exist beyond the bonds of space
coordinated and extended
Without space and time

Know yourself, but swiftly, you who
passionately yearn[138]
So that you may discover the secrets of existence
You shall find the "Unseen"[139]

---

138. The dictum, "Know thyself" in the case of the Delphic Oracle, is found in countless sources. It is found in the Prophetic *Hadīth*: "He who knows himself, knows his Lord." See, for example, Bukhārī's, *Sahih.*

All your senses[140] and all your apprehensions
Are but mere tools for your essence
Your I-ness is not for just a bodily tool

You who are neither [given] to speculation, specific
     will, nor judgment skills
For you such things will cause "I-ness"-you-become
     manifest, thus your Evidenz-identity
     recognized
Do you know who you really are? Light's essence!

139. The Qur'ān clearly distinguishes between the "Unseen" and the "seen" worlds. Only God is privy to "Knowledge of the Unseen," *al-qayb*. For example, "to God alone belongs the Unseen" (X, 20). This is constant and does not vary, not even His Chosen are privy to "Knowledge of the Unseen."
140. *ihsās* (sensations) and *idrāk* (apprehensions) are technical terms employed to convey levels of "knowing".

Go, seek the real cause, not what are passing causes
Go, look inside the house, not linger at the door
Go, find a real soul, one aware of realities

Go seek faqr, *pass away from this repository of dirt*
Step onto the zenith of the seventh heaven
Then, soar extended space at the apogee of
     lā makān,[141] *yet travel even beyond*
The Qurʾānic statement, "I am the Creator", is real
     — We the referents
"We have no knowledge",[142] refers to others
Does ignorance suit you?

141. See fn. 14, 62.
142. Many Qurʾānic *āyas* refer to those "who have no knowledge," for example: XXIV, 19, but they are too numerous to be listed.

Ponder deeply that which you fathom: definition,
description, and dimension in that space
with such, nor any other qualifiers
As for the unchanging, unmoving things,
choose true vision
So that your certitude will increase

The Absolute Essence of Being has no limit
Whose name in human language of
discourse is "God"
Words are different from meaning

Our logic speaks of the Essence
The limited unit is a generality
Suitable to the senses

The secret of existence is no doubt the verse:
"Everything perishes, save His Visage"[143]
None is eternal but He

All existent-ness of Holistic Being
Is the same as the unlimited absolute Act
Including all being, and all "appearing"

143. *Wajh-i Allāh*, God's Visage (some use "Countenance"); for example, Muhammad Marmaduke Pickthal, whose bilingual edition is
widely used. The foundations are all in the Qurʾān. The term *wajh*
without suffixation, but not only in the nominative case, appears in
11 *āyas*; 5 times in construct state with Allah, *Wajhu Allāh i*; but in 2
of the 5: II, 115; and II, 272; the basic meanings are: God's Visage is
everywhere — of great importance to Sufism — ; and to seek God's
Visage is a good thing; in 2 of them there is no mention of the equivalent of the "Beatific Vision"; in 2 of the 11 the term is in construct
with "Lord", *rabb* (XIII, 22 & IC, 20), where the base meaning is that
His Visage shall remain while all else in the cosmos will perish. The
specific reference in this verse is to XXVIII, 88. This latter meaning is
also found in the Oral Tradition.

He, the Exalted Lord God

Rise, for unless you do not break away

from the corporeal self, you shall not

find salvation

And, if you shall not abandon your

selfhood's colorful shape, you shall not

find salvation

When, you become freed from selfhood,

then you shall become everything

But, if anything of your external being

remains, you shall not be freed.

The seventh dimension is the divine Empyrean
"lā" and "illā" exist not there
In that "Place", "there" is merely Oneness

The "Throne", the "Tablet" and the "Pen"
    are pre-eternal
At every turn, it is fate that commands them
In reality, it is the same as free will

The eternal scroll has no beginning
Yet, it contains each and every event with no
    attention as to when they occurred
Written all the way up a path without an
    upper bound

On the unscratched Tabula Rasa of the human,
 He struck a "pen"
He did so at the instant of time,[144] eternal and
 without spatial extensions
Exactly as God ordained, nothing added,
 nothing less

The Sufi's soul will become known at such a
 "moment"
He has turned his face from all but the
 Compassionate
The heart's throne he has ripped asunder
 [with his knowledge]

144. Dam — The concept of time beyond our earthly "measure of distance", which Aristotle had defined, dominating science until recently. In Sufism the idea of a type of "durationless time", that extended, was available since a millennia. Thus, here in the second hemistich — "dam", a moment of time without dimension — the author draws upon a long tradition of non-Aristotelian science and philosophy.

God does not in reality journey,

For, what can a voyage be to Him who has no other

Existence is nothing but the Good

Wherever Existence showed off Itself

Then know that night there is the very reason for the

[Aristotelian] ten categories not to be real

To say nothing of "quantity" & "quality"

[both categories]

There is no difference between Form and Prime

Matter[145]

The difference is slight [to the naked eye]

but substantial to the physicist

Do not dwell on this meaning

145. In Greek Physics, Prime Matter (*heyole*, Persianised *hayūla*) plus Form, the latter as pure Potentiality, are the foundations of the corporeal reality at least.

Otherwise, the image of capacity to perfection
Would be inscribed upon the age's Tablet
Keep away from idle chatter and talk

Yet immature cogitative minds
Think of, and name, all incomparable stones: "gem"!
Obscuring your day's thinking

The [wayfarer does] journey among many
   distinct points
How can any of what we have actually done be
   related to God?
His elevated deportment is far superior — it is

Since the "unlimited" realm has no
"empty quarters" [146]
Therefore, the journey in being is a deduction based
on no "Principle"
But, Based upon what is the "gushing forth
of being" [147]

The absolute Essence is not given to "flux" [148]
How can a self-existent entity, be dearth?
I shall indicate a point, [explaining
"self-constituted"]

146. The author's principle view concerning the Gnostic's Cosmos is that it is a continuum whole, and without bounds. Thus, there can be no "empty quarters." In mathematics it can be proven that certain types of continuous functions have no singularities-roughly parallel to the author's poetic statement.

147. Plotinus' novel, *The Enneades* (*Tāsūʿāt* in Arabic) had a great impact on Islamic thought. Two editions exist of the Arabic Books IV & V and a few statements commonly believed to be the only extant version, or, the only parts actually put to Arabic. "Gushing forth" used here by the author, is the manner Plotinus describes the process "becoming."

148. Flux is a pre-Socratic concept: all things in the universe move and change.

Bodily changes are subordinate to your essence
"Rest" as well as "moving" are your interpretations
They simply are descriptions of your apprehension

It is simply your own false judgment concerning
      motion and rest
But, such findings were simple falsities in terms
      of essence
Essence is beyond condition

The foundations of science are probable
Are not the same truth, in agreement with custom
Nor relying on popular statements

The [term] "awe"[149] *[is a consequence of acts of the*
  inner sense] phantasia;[150]*makes the*
  "probable" be dismissed
[On the other hand], "Sobriety"[151] *is indeed known:*
  the Essence of God Almighty
Into what you pervade, through this [poetic]
  discourse

The Principles[152] *of the Known*[153] *[knowledge &*
  the way] are not based upon "the unknown"
All shapes, images and things the [Faculty] fantasy
  bring to mind, are nothing other than
  fabrication.[154]
And, no one apprehends this intellectually

149. Awe is one of the states (*ahwāl*) as well as stages (*maqāmā*t) of
Sufi psychology of "inner" soul.
150. One of the Five Inner Faculties of the mind is signified by the
Greek *phantasia*.
151. "Sobriety," *sahw*, opposite "intoxication," *sukr*.
152. The Persian, *pāyeh*, is used synonymously with the Arabic, ʿ*asl*,
in the language of intellectual discourse, poetry and prose. The most

What you create are pure [base-less] fabrications
How could the Known ever be pure fantasy?
Behold! What a difference between this
　　　　and pure essence

"God is the Cause of Causes" [said Aristotle]
Do not dwell on such idle talk, for Being is Absolute
And, Absolute Being is God

intricate signification of the terms is "Primary Principles of Epistemological Process."
153. The term used here, *maʿlūm*, is one of the primary ones (at the
core) of the language of intellectual discourse in Iran, and it has been
steadily defined and re-defined in the process of refining and aug-
menting philosophy and other intellectual endeavor in Iran (Persianised Arabic plus Persian; which is a combination giving it an
almost unique force) from the 11th-12th centuries to the present.
154. The term *majhūl*, unknown, is the technical term opposite, or
contradictory to the term, *maʿlūm*.

Reality Emanated upon the Ocean of Existence is
wholly Evident[155]
The secret of Being is just this: "God is Light!"[156]
And, Moses did see the Light on Mount Sinai

There is nothing lacking nor defiant in the
emanation of the Light
But of Light's Presence, one without proper ability
to see, is unaware
Although he's not far from it

155. The technical German phenomenological term was previously used to indicate the degree of equivocal luminosity caused by the light which has propagated the Islamic Peripatetic term which is problematic. Thus "Existence is wholly Evident" is due to the most intense degree of luminosity of the light, and here *Evidenz* could be replaced by *Manifest*, but, as indicated earlier, *Evidenz* so exactly conveys the signification of the term *Zuhūr*, chosen to be more exact than common.

156. The expression "God is Light" is in clear reference to the signification(s) of the term "light", *nūr*, in the Qur'ān. The term *nūr* appears in 24 *āyas* in the nominative case. In 23 of them "light" is in opposition to darkness and associated with the Bad and the Evil. Both are God's Creation (in the case of darkness, the term "made" is used instead of "created," but this does not change the signification. E. g.: VI, 1). In 22 verses of the 24 God aids humankind to "come out" of

The light of the real sun openly reveals truths
Bats — and Bat-likes — do not see it, though
Become an Attribute and share "sameness"
  with the Essence

This universe is permeated with God's Grace
  through emanation
Only in the inner may one seek the life secret
Become as Essence manifest in attribute

Words as: "The womb of the womb", "The veil's
  veil" are idle talk
Absolute Being is beyond any "naming"
How you benefit from this all depends on you

darkness; to leave darkness and thus find faith etc. For example: II,
257; V, 16; XIV, 1; etc. And humankind finds solace away from darkness in light. There is, however, one *Sūra* in the Qurʾān named *Sūrat
al-Nūr* (XXIV), and has been the subject of much discussion among
often opposing Muslim views. Especially XXIV, 35: "God is the Light
of the Heavens and the Earth, His Light is similar to a niche wherein
is a lamp . . ."

The Essence and the pure Absolute Being the same,
    they are
This is why I stated that it is Absolute Being
Essence is beyond these words

This Chanteh in total "faqr" and despondency
To the Beloved's Throne I took as a "gift"
May it be that He finds value worthy unto it.

❖ ❖ ❖ ❖

Appendices

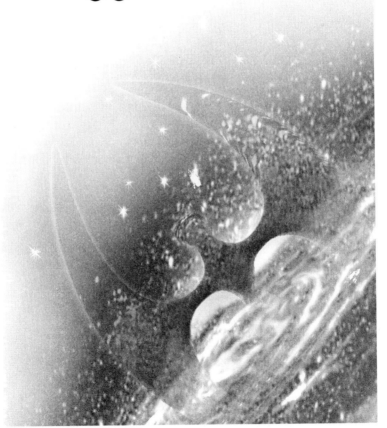

Appendix I: Genealogy of
M.T.O. Shahmaghsoudi *(School of Islamic Sufism)*®

Prophet Mohammad
Imam Ali
1. Hazrat Oveys Gharani*
2. Hazrat Salman Farsi
3. Hazrat Habib-ibn Salim Ra'i
4. Hazrat Soltan Ebrahim Adham
5. Hazrat Abu Ali Shaqiq al-Balkhi
6. Hazrat Sheikh Abu Torab Nakhshabi
7. Hazrat Sheikh Abi Amr al-Istakhri
8. Hazrat Abu Ja'far Hazza
9. Hazrat Sheikh Kabir Abu Abdollah Mohammad-ibn Khafif Shirazi
10. Hazrat Sheikh Hossein Akkar
11. Hazrat Sheikh Morshed Abu-Isshaq Shahriar Kazerouni
12. Hazrat Khatib Abolfath Abdolkarim
13. Hazrat Ali-ibn Hassan Basri
14. Hazrat Serajeddin Abolfath Mahmoud-ibn Mahmoudi Sabouni Beyzavi
15. Hazrat Sheikh Abu Abdollah Rouzbehan Baghli Shirazi
16. Hazrat Sheikh Najmeddin Tamat-al Kobra Khivaghi
17. Hazrat Sheikh Ali Lala Ghaznavi
18. Hazrat Sheikh Ahmad Zaker Jowzeghani
19. Hazrat Noureddin Abdolrahman Esfarayeni
20. Hazrat Sheikh Alaoddowleh Semnani
21. Hazrat Mahmoud Mazdaghani
22. Hazrat Amir Seyyed Ali Hamedani
23. Hazrat Sheikh Ahmad Khatlani
24. Hazrat Seyyed Mohammad Abdollah Ghatifi al-Hasavi Nourbakhsh
25. Hazrat Shah Ghassem Feyzbakhsh
26. Hazrat Hossein Abarghoui Janbakhsh
27. Hazrat Darvish Malek Ali Joveyni
28. Hazrat Darvish Ali Sodeyri
29. Hazrat Darvish Kamaleddin Sodeyri
30. Hazrat Darvish Mohammad Mozaheb Karandehi (Pir Palandouz)
31. Hazrat Mir Mohammad Mo'men Sodeyri Sabzevari
32. Hazrat Mir Mohammad Taghi Shahi Mashhadi
33. Hazrat Mir Mozaffar Ali
34. Hazrat Mir Mohammad Ali
35. Hazrat Seyyed Shamseddin Mohammad
36. Hazrat Seyyed Abdolvahab Naini
37. Hazrat Haj Mohammad Hassan Kouzekanani
38. Hazrat Agha Abdolghader Jahromi
39. Hazrat Jalaleddin Ali Mir Abolfazl Angha
40. Hazrat Mir Ghotbeddin Mohammad Angha
41. Hazrat Molana Shah Maghsoud Sadegh Angha
42. Hazrat Salaheddin Ali Nader Shah Angha

The conventional Arabic transliteration is Uwais al-Qarani

Appendix II: Partial works by the Author

Molana Shah Maghsoud Sadegh Angha, *"Pir Oveyssi"* has written well over 150 books, treatises, essays and other works on *Irfan* in prose and verse conveyed through different disciplines. These include:

	Written	First Published
Psalm of the Gods	1955	1963
Iron	1950	1950
Principles of Faghr & Sufism	1974	1987
The Sufi Miracle — Commentary on the Holy Qur'an (11 volumes)	1962-1977*	
Owzan va Mizan (Weights and Balance)	1972	1973
Stages of Cognition in the Holy Qur'an	1972	1973
Manifestations of Thought	1950	1954
Message from the Soul	1960	1968
The Human Magnetic Body	1970	forthcoming
The Complete Arithmomancy	1967	forthcoming
Chanteh — Realm of the Sufi	1940	1943
Life	1970	forthcoming
Microbic Sages	1951	1951
Two Pulse Beats	1973	forthcoming
Remembrance	1965	forthcoming
Al-Salat	1978	1978
Purification & Enlightenment of Hearts	1978	1978
The Light of Salvation	1978	1978
The States of Enlightenment	1978	1978
The Hidden Angles of Life	1972	1974
Serr-ol Hajar	1960	1983
The Stages of the Seeker and the Ascent of Nader	1966	1983
The Mantle's Lineage	1945	1945
Through the Gates of the Unseen	1966	1983
The Traditional Medicine of Iran	1976	1978
Love and Fate	1938	1938
The Science of Numbers	1961	forthcoming
The Science of Names	1962	forthcoming
The Science of Coordinates and Squares	1962	forthcoming
The Principles of Oneness (The Epic of Life)	1966	1968
Ghazaliat	1960	1984
The Star in Literature	1931	1932
Kymya	1961	1972
Golzar-e Omid (The Flowers of Hope)	1963	1964
Nader's Treasure	(1940-1979)*	
The Rightful Visions	1970	forthcoming
Psalms of Truth	1962	1964
Nirvan	1955	1960
Heavenly Colors	1960	1984

being compiled

Chanteh —
the
Gnostic's Cosmos

REVEALED

In Order to assist the seeker,
Molana Shah Maghsoud Sadegh Angha
included his comments in prose
for each section of the book
in original Farsi.
These textual comments have been
translated and is being published.